T0196082

# LET HIM THAT SLEEPETH

## *Arise*

A. I. UZEBU

**WESTBOW**
P R E S S®
A DIVISION OF THOMAS NELSON
& ZONDERVAN

WestBow Press books may be ordered through booksellers or by contacting:

WestBow Press
A Division of Thomas Nelson & Zondervan
1663 Liberty Drive
Bloomington, IN 47403
www.westbowpress.com
1 (866) 928-1240

Unless stated otherwise, all Scripture quotations are taken from the King James Version.

Scripture quotations marked NKJV are taken from the New King James Version®. Copyright © 1982 by Thomas Nelson. Used by permission. All rights reserved.

ISBN: 978-1-9736-8977-5 (sc)
ISBN: 978-1-9736-8976-8 (hc)
ISBN: 978-1-9736-8978-2 (e)

Library of Congress Control Number: 2020907079

Print information available on the last page.

WestBow Press rev. date: 5/11/2020

# ELOHIM OUR GOD (EOG) MINISTRIES

## SUNDAY 11th, 2017

Prophet Aiyudubie Israel Uzebu

# Contents

# ১ 1 ২

## Introduction

Unto whom it was revealed, that not unto themselves, but unto us they did minister the things, which are now reported unto you by them that have preached the gospel unto you with the Holy Ghost sent down from heaven; which things the angels desire to look into. Wherefore gird up the loins of your mind, be sober, and hope to the end for the grace that is to be brought unto you at the revelation of Jesus Christ; As obedient children, not fashioning yourselves according to the former lusts in your ignorance: But as he which hath called you is holy, so be ye holy in all manner of conversation. (1 Peter 1:12–15)

The word of God tells us to be sober and alert; this admonishing is to engender us who walk this earth to have a mind-set that we are sojourners upon it. We as believers in Christ Jesus are to be mindful of our daily doings and goings in these last days. Our adversary- Satan and the powers of darkness- are out to cause many to fall out of the way of faith. The only way that this can take place is when we yield ourselves to their enticements and seduction, which are clearly lies. Yielding leads to spiritual sleep and slumbering.

Spiritual sleep or slumber is a state of mind wherein the consciousness is suppressed into doing that which is against God's word. Remember that anything that goes contrary to the will of God is in enmity with Him. The intention of God is to awaken believers from that state of mind imposed on their senses by sin and disobedience to the light of truth and love.

First John 4:7–8 clearly states that God is love and that those who love belong to God and know their creator. Knowing the creator and embracing his light create in you the power of spiritual alertness and strength to overcome the trials and temptations of this world. Trials and temptations are things that we all must pass through. Just like in a car factory, before each vehicle is released for sales, it must first be tested and tried. Each car that meets all the criteria is sent forward into the market. So also, our testing is necessary to bring out that quality and to make us perfect; just as our Father in heaven is perfect. Our God is a holy God and demands that those who pass through this earth, focusing on Jesus Christ, should by the power of the Holy Spirit come out holy just like him.

Spiritual sleep or slumber is a serious issue as it has plagued our communities, homes, churches, schools, and indeed our world. Spiritual sleep is a scary and tragic situation. You as a believer working in the light of truth need not be afraid, as you can remember what our Lord and Savior Jesus Christ spoke of regarding these days. To give us a clear understanding of the spiritual state of mind of many people, the Lord stated that his return shall be like "a thief in the night." This word allows us to grasp how ready the world will be upon his return. With respect to their spiritual state of mind, many people shall be asleep.

When people are naturally asleep, their consciousness is suspended from surrounding activities. This is the reason why some people get their faces painted while they have snoozed-off in the classroom or at office. Not that this is a good thing to do; however, it demonstrates how sleeping suspends the mind from the natural senses. In the spiritual perspective of sleep, the eyes are open and not closed; but the spiritual senses are disconnected. This is the reason each and every believer must strive to be spiritually awake and alert. Spiritual awakening is the intention of God for the last days; therefore, I encourage you to be sober and be vigilant (alert).

# ❧ 2 ❧

# What Is the Meaning of Sleep?

*Therefore He says:*

*"Awake, you who sleep,*
*Arise from the dead*
*And Christ will give you light."*
*(Ephesians 5:14 NKJV)*

What is the meaning of sleep? *Sleep, slept,* and *sleeping* are forms of a verb (used without object). To sleep means to take a certain kind of rest that results in the suspension of voluntary bodily functions and the natural suspension, complete or partial, of consciousness; ceasing from being awake (Webster Dictionary).

*Sleep* is a verb, and a verb is an action word. Sleeping can be voluntary, and it is a natural action that, when undertaken, causes people to suspend their consciousness. Consciousness refers to awareness or a sensory response to a matter, so that it can be acknowledged to exist. Acknowledgment depends on attention, and attention and focus are the play of the mind. For you to truly apprehend and appreciate whatever is being presented before you, you must be in a conscious state.

Wakefulness also does not necessarily mean we are paying attention. Our attention or focus still needs to be directed toward the object presented, so that it can be recorded into our consciousness. Once we are conscious of it, we are now able to analyze and appreciate what is before us.

In the matter of attention and focus, we are all guilty of paying attention to some certain thing around us, while we neglect other matters, even though they are right in front of us. This is the power of the brain and senses. The brain can sometimes eliminate things that it senses to be unimportant; while it helps us focus on those that are important. Have you driven down a road leading to your house so many times that you never took note of a certain thing—not until you were looking for something around that place? As your attention was drawn to that location and the suppression of brain cues was eliminated, you were suddenly able to see a store, a poster, a statue, or something you never acknowledged to exist. This is the power that the brain has on our perception by means of directing our attention to sense and interpret the things around us.

When sleep is the state during which attention and consciousness are analyzed, a sleeping person may have a degree of consciousness but will never be able to demonstrate attention. Attention requires wakefulness; and without attention there is no consciousness. In the Christian faith, if you are a follower of Jesus Christ and are spiritually asleep, this means that you not paying attention and have lost consciousness.

Your focus and attention as a believing Christian must be on Jesus Christ; however, when the spiritual mind has been corrupted, then the power for attention is lost. Spiritual sleep is the opposite of spiritual wakefulness. When you are spiritually awake, it means that your spiritual self has been revived to life through the power and word of life, Jesus Christ. Spiritual sleep makes you care less for the things of God, and it diminishes your faith in Jesus Christ, if you ever had faith. Spiritual sleep makes you more yielded and comfortable with sin, disobedience, and anything that is totally against God and his word.

> Wherefore he saith, Awake thou that sleepest, and arise from the dead, and Christ shall give thee light. (Ephesians 5:14)

Ephesians 5:14 exhorts anyone who is caught up in spiritual sleep (ungodliness, disobedience, or transgression) to awaken from that slumber (suspension of consciousness) and become conscious (submit to the authority, will, and power of God). Jesus Christ said to his disciples, as he is speaking to everybody; "If any want to be with me, they need to deny themselves, pick up the cross, and follow me" (Matthew 16:24, paraphrased). When you choose not to sin, you are choosing to remain awake; in the contrary state, you yield to the seductions of Satan.

Just as Adam and Eve were tempted in the Garden of Eden, so also was Jesus Christ tempted; however, he chose not to yield to the seducing power of Satan. Jesus Christ was born and raised just as we all are, but he chose to follow after God in his heart and denied himself the pleasures, lust, and things that the world uses to lure people away from the faith. His actions earned him the power for spiritual wakefulness and consciousness; and he received from God power and authority.

For you to experience wakefulness, you must follow in the

footsteps of holiness, righteousness, and truth, denying yourself just as Jesus Christ did. The outcome of self-denial is spiritual awakening and experiencing the light of the power of God. According to Ephesians 5:14, "Christ will give you light."

Jesus Christ is the light of God. He is a light to the world so that all who walk in darkness should find their way to true love and be saved from the destruction and wrath of God to come upon this world—that is, everybody who has not followed the truth. Jesus Christ is the Son of God and a gift of salvation to all people. As the last and final hope and gift for salvation, God's intention is that whosoever believes in him shall be saved (John 3:16) from the curse that was imposed on us by our ancestors (Adam and Eve). In addition, God's intention is that through the sacrificial blood of Jesus Christ shared on the cross of Calvary, the curse imposed on us by our ancestors shall be washed away (Isaiah 1:18). For you to be saved and transformed from a state of ungodly nature (spiritual sleep and slumber) to a godly state (spiritually awake), you need the light of God to shine into your life through Jesus Christ, who is the way, the truth, and the life—the hope of glory.

# 3

## The Psychophysiology Definition of Sleep

There are 5 cycles of sleep. 4 are called none rapid eye movement (NREM) and 1 rapid eye movement (REM)

- Beta
- Alpha
- Theta
- Spindle
- Delta

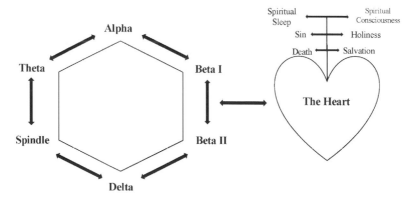

FIGURE 1: THE 5 SPIRITUAL SLEEP LEVELS

The sleep cycle in the scientific sense is a pattern that each individual passes through during sleep. This pattern or cycle is divided into five stages, and the main source of sleep control is from the hypothalamus, a segment of the brain. The hypothalamus is responsible for shutting down the brain's arousal signals, which results in sleep. The *medulla oblongata*, another part of the brain, also plays a role in arousal and consciousness. The part of the medulla oblongata that regulates sleep and consciousness is called the *reticular formation*. The medulla oblongata controls breathing as well. Any damage to this part of the brain, depending on the intensity of damage, leads to coma or death. This area of the brain also contains many nerves called ascending and descending fibers, which carry and relay neural information between our brain and body.

As noted earlier in regard to the five sleep stages, the deepest level of sleep is called the beta stage. Second, the main source of sleep control comes from the midbrain, and it does have a strong influence on the level of consciousness. In addition to sleeping cycle and wakefulness, the natural sleep patterns are all created by God. The first-time sleep is mentioned in the Holy Bible is the time Adam was put to sleep by God with an intention to create. It is written: "And the Lord caused a deep sleep to fall upon Adam, and he slept: and he took one of his ribs, and closed up the flesh instead thereof" (Genesis 2:21). The scripture used the words *he slept* to emphasize the depth of sleep and loss of physical and spiritual consciousness. The Lord had to suspend his consciousness in order to bring into existence another being, Eve. This was a positive sleep, because its product is the bringing into existence the will and power of God (Eve).

The level of consciousness decreases as the level of sleep increases, and the power of attention declines to zero. Just as natural sleep needs you to decide whether to engage in the act, so also with spiritual sleep. The similarity between the spiritual and natural sleep is that you have the power and will to go into that state of little to no consciousness. Therefore, you can also decide to go into spiritual sleep. The difference between them is the consequence of the sleep, as one is beneficial, and the other is detrimental.

## $\mathcal{W}$hat Are Spiritual Consciousness and Unconsciousness?

What are spiritual consciousness and unconsciousness in respect to the Christian faith? Spiritual consciousness is grounded in obedience to God's word and following Jesus Christ. Spiritual consciousness is based on love for the truth and for God. The Bible states that "true Love conquers and cleanses (1 Peter 4:8)"; furthermore, "through love and faithfulness sin is atoned for; through the fear of the Lord evil is avoided" (Proverbs 16:6 NIV).

The level of consciousness of Christians (believers) is also based on their awareness of God's power, God's purpose, who Jesus Christ is and why he died; why they are here on Earth; and their faithfulness, righteousness, and holiness. Spiritual consciousness comes from the convicting power of God working in you. It is the power of God that fortifies you with the knowledge and understanding for the knowing of God's plan and promise.

Those who walk in love as Jesus Christ did are walking in the light of truth. It is the light of truth that awakens you. The light of truth, which is the power of God, working in you is what enhances your love for God and hatred toward sin. First John 4:7 (KJV) states that "Beloved, let us love on another: for love is of God;

and everyone that loveth is born of God, and knoweth God." Wherever there exists a restraint in the expression or sharing of love, such a place is the dwelling of darkness; and in such a place the people are observed to operate at the unconscious spiritual state of mind.

Not to digress away from the description of the occurrences taking place at each level of the sleep cycle (stages), the beta level is divided into two, and is experienced at the beginning of the cycle and at the last level of the sleep cycle. The beta stages are somewhat closer to consciousness, and this fact is what distinguishes it from the other stages. It is unique because it is easy to bring the person at that stage of sleep back to a conscious level through external stimuli. At this stage of the sleep cycle one can choose to remain in sleep (unconsciousness) or choose to go into a wakeful state (consciousness).

Many Christians (believers) are at this stage spiritually, which makes it somewhat pragmatic. Strange as it sounds, this near-conscious level of sleep is present both in the physical sleep and spiritual sleep. Spiritual wakefulness and a sleeping state of mind are the two choices with respect to your walk with God. Many believers are simply comfortable with the beta stage and prefer to avoid full commitment of their lives to Jesus Christ. Some people are just afraid of knowing the truth or getting involved in the matters that involve being a true believer. These people are not strong in their faith with God and would rather remain in a state of spiritual suspension.

Satan is the father of all lies, fears, and deceptions. Satan has in countless ways seduced people into a sleep state without them knowing that they are spiritually asleep. Spiritual sleep is what makes you feel comfortable with sin and even encourage others to do or indulge in it. Spiritual sleep can also drive your destiny in the directions that God never intended it to go. Spiritual sleep brings compromise and acceptance of lies. Spiritual sleep or slumber arouses in you the power for total submission and conformity to things that are clearly not of Jesus Christ. Spiritual sleep or slumber is what make you to start to fight against the truth and the word of God. Spiritual sleep or slumber makes you hate people who stand for the truth.

A spiritual state of unconsciousness creates unawareness and serves Satan as an instrument for luring people into deeper darkness. Sometimes the luring may come in a relationship, a business, a promotion, a gift, or something that Satan knows you like. I say this out of experience and what I have personally observed Satan and the power of darkness doing to many believers. The loss of a spiritual state of attention and consciousness can only occur when you allow Satan to walk into your life and your heart. Remember, Satan was an angel of light (Lucifer), and when you allow him to take possession of your heart, he will take over and will try to put you into the sleep state. However, this won't take place unless you yield through your actions. Whenever you don't yield to Satan, he will move away and will yet try other means (Matthew 12:43–45; Luke 11:24).

In other words, you need to pay attention and be sober minded (1 Peter 5:8–9) because Satan, our adversary, is seeking those he may devour. Your mind has to be fixed on Jesus Christ, and you must have a genuine love for God. As guanine love is what will keep you from falling out of the way. When you have true love that cannot be shaken, it becomes difficult for Satan to lure you into a lesser state of consciousness. When your faith is not compromising but rather strong as a rock, you become unmalleable and unshakable just like Jesus Christ when he was tempted by Satan.

Those who have compromised their faith are in both the beta stages. The spiritual beta stages, as stated earlier, are found at the extreme ends of the sleep cycle. There is some similarity between them. The people in the spiritual beta stages entered by choice. The difference between them is the choices made before going into such a state. The people in the first spiritual beta stage (B-1) still retain their belief in Jesus Christ, which means that they once were in the state of consciousness. These people have lost the power to pay attention because their eyes are closed to the truth voluntarily; however, their spiritual senses are not entirely suspended. They can be aroused as a redirecting and soundly invigorating move by the Holy Spirit comes over them.

On the other hand, people in the second beta stage (B-2) deny Jesus Christ and have completely backslidden. These people have their senses suspended and can be awakened from sleep by little external stimulation and redirecting them to the word of the Lord for obedience.

Not all states of spiritual sleep are entered by choice consciously; some people are born into such a state of spiritual sleep or slumber. In other words, a state of spiritual suspension can be voluntary (by choice) or involuntary (not by choice). These people were born involuntarily into the sleep state; however, they remain in that state by choice. For this reason, their choice of spiritual unconsciousness is still punishable by God, because it is made by choice. Implicitly, in Figure 1, people in the Beta stages at one time or another in their lives experienced the state of consciousness. Furthermore, these people currently are fully aware of their spiritual state and walk with God. People in the other stages (B-2) find themselves at that level due to circumstances.

I remember meeting a man in New York who was a drunkard

and had a smell of old alcohol and urine all over him. I had a night shift job, and every night he would walk past me to solicit the prostitutes or buy more alcohol. One day I walked up to him and struck up a conversation with him. While talking with me, he told me that I came from a Christian home. This same man also told me about my mother, that she was a prayerful person and much more. Upon further questioning, he told me that he once had been a pastor and owned a church. I preached to him and encouraged him to come back, but he refused and said that God would not forgive him. The drunkard told me God had given him the spirit of prophecy and discernment; and he could tell people about their lives, when he still was walking in the light of faith and truth. There are also many people who were abused and hurt, and as a result of this inflicting experiences in their life the power of darkness and Satan is keeping them away from the truth, through lies, fear, hatred, and unforgiveness. For this reason, these same people will sometime show hatred to Christians and believers who are walking in the pathway of truth. Such people become tools for advocating and expanding the work of Satan.

I know the question may have stoke your mind as to "how possible is the fact that this man is still prophesying and discerning despite having fallen away from the pathway of righteousness and truth?" He is able to express this spiritual gift because God will not take away the things he has imparted to any person or spirit (vessel), even if they turn away from him. This is also true about Satan (Lucifer) and the angels who were cast out of heaven with him. Satan still possesses the power that God gave him when he was created, and it has not been taken away from him. This is the reason Satan and the power of darkness can carry out certain activities, even posing as an angel of God to deceive people.

The gift of God is without repentance (see Romans 11:29), and unless you turn back and ask for forgiveness, you will continue to walk in a state of diminished consciousness. Just as those taking natural sleep still possess their strengths and abilities while sleeping, so also is the spiritual sleep. For this reason, the drunken man on the New York street was still able to tell me about my mother and certain other things using the gift God had imparted into his life for the operation of his(God) own will and purpose.

# 4

## What Is Spiritual Sleep or Slumber?

*Hear this now, O foolish people,*
*Without understanding,*
*Who have eyes and see not,*
*and who have ears and hear not.*
*(Jeremiah 5:21 NKJV)*

*This people's heart is waxed gross, and their*
*ears are dull of hearing, and their eyes they*
*have closed; lest at any time they should see with*
*their eyes and hear with their ears, and should*
*understand with their heart, and should be*
*converted, and I should heal them. (Matthew*
*13:15 KJV)*

Jeremiah was a Prophet of God sent to the people of Judah, as
Judah was separated from Israel, to warn them of God's judgment
and punishment (Jeremiah 7:1-34) that would come if the people

did not change their ways and repent from their sins and come back to God (2 Chronicles 7:14). The Lord said to the Prophet that these people will not repent, nor obey the warning sent through Jeremiah. The people at that time forgot about God's commandment and were lost in their busy lifestyle; they bowed and worshipped idols and enacted even more immoralities than the people whom God drove out of the land he gave to them as an inheritance. Due to their sins and transgression against his commandment and laws, God was angry with them (Israel and Judah) and sent many Prophets and messengers—to no avail, because they did not obey.

According to the Book of Jeremiah the Prophet, the people forgot about God and his commandments (Deuteronomy chapters 6–8). The people of Israel and Judah were seduced, and out of lust, they sought powers from other gods and made sacrifices to idols and the gods of the people whom God drove out from the lands. Reflecting on the time of the Prophets of Judah and Israel, and comparing it to what is happening around us today, you will see that we are currently on that verge of the mercy of God. When you look deep and search through the Holy Scriptures, there is nothing done today that was not done at that time, including seeking pleasures and satiating lust. The spiritual description of what took place is that these people went into a state of spiritual sleep and slumber and backsliding.

> Hear this now, O foolish people,
> Without understanding,
> Who have eyes and see not,
> And who have ears and hear not.
> (Jeremiah 5:21 NKJV)

All the commandment of God is based on one entity—that is, *love*. In other words, to truly gain divine understanding, one must seek to love God. When you love God and embrace the truth, with this action comes the power of understanding. When people seek after what pleases them and put God to the side, this leads them to the pathway of destruction and away from the love of God. Where there is no understanding, the people perish (Proverbs 29:18). Understanding comes from God. With understanding is the power to fulfill God's will and purpose for your life. Within the will of God is the divine vision for your life. When there is no understanding, there is no vision, and the people will perish. They perish because they have entered a state defined as spiritual suspension of consciousness (Jeremiah 5:21). The state of spiritual sleep and slumbering is what Jeremiah was describing as written in the Holy Scripture.

Natural sleep is a gift that God gave to every creature in order that they get refreshment and rest their body from daily labor. During sleep, metaphysical events are taking place in the body and in the brain (mind). For this reason, people who don't get enough sleep often find themselves moody or not functioning properly. Therefore, we must all sleep at some time or other, in the natural sense and for the purpose our God created it. On the other hand, the course of spiritual sleep and slumber runs contrary. Expanding on the referenced scripture (Jeremiah 5:21), it states that their eyes are open, but they can't see; the ears are fully open, but they can't hear; they have a brain, but there is no understanding because their heart has been corrupted. The spiritual nature of these individuals is clearly not functioning even though they are in place; and their spiritual senses are suspended from the truth and the word of God. Suspension is taking place because they have lost contact with the basis which is grounded in the love of God.

> On the seventh day God ended his work which he had made; and he rested on the seventh day from all his work which he had made. And God blessed the seventh day, and sanctified it: because that in it he had rested from all his work which God created and made. (Genesis 2:2–3)

According to the Book of Genesis, God rested on the seventh day. Remember also that it was also mentioned in **Genesis (1:27)** that we were created in the image and likeness of God. Therefore, natural sleeping in the natural sense is a good thing, and according to research, a lot of physiological processes including growth, repairs, and replenishing of energy, all take place mostly when we sleep (Dowshen, 2017). Spiritual sleep on the other hand is not so. Spiritual sleep impairs spiritual consciousness, but the subject is fully awake (not caught up in the natural sleep).

The purpose of spiritual sleep is to impair judgment and prevent the natural course of God's purpose and will. If spiritual sleep goes against the will of God, it must simply mean that although natural sleep affords us rejuvenation, spiritual sleep brings death and the wrath (judgment) of God. When we observe natural sleep, we discover certain phenomena called dreams. Dreams in themselves are a powerful tool and a topic on their own. Dreams can only occur when our natural senses and consciousness are suspended; and they occur at the sleep levels called delta and beta.

Spiritual visions are similar to dreams, but those who

experience them are not sleeping or closing their eyes. God sometimes use visions and dreams to communicate to people. In spiritual sleep the eyes can see what is happening, but the willpower to resist sin and the willpower to obey God's instruction have been impaired.

Jesus Christ wept many times for those around him (because they were locked in a state of spiritual sleep and slumber) and for Jerusalem (Matthew 23:33–39). The sight of people in such a state of spiritual suspension was unbearable. Many people around us find themselves in this state of spiritual suspension with no awareness they are in such a state. The state of spiritual sleep is totally deceptive. Instead of being a natural sleep, spiritual sleep or slumber is rather an entrapment and entanglement by Satan and the powers of darkness in order that people will not awaken to the truth. Spiritual sleep, just like a leash on an animal, can restrain its victim from yielding themselves to the Word of God. These people see nothing wrong with what they are doing. In their spiritual and natural minds' eye, they are doing everything right.

The agenda of the powers of darkness is to keep people unconscious, which is a lower state of mind, in order that their soul might not be saved. These are people who just wake up one day, even with everything going well around them, and feel sad, lonely, depressed, and empty. Some are those you see or hear of on the TV or radio as having committed suicide. Some of these people may also identify themselves to be Christians. That is why when you, an awakened Christian, observing these people and what they are doing, you start to ponder on hows and whys. The fact is that you will never understand what is pushing them in such a pathway unless the Holy Spirit gives a clear understanding.

Walking in the path of truth affords you access to the power of God. It is the power of God working in your life that gives you understanding. Remember that the opposite of understanding is confusion. Confusion is the agenda of Satan, and it is one of the tools that he is using today to seduce people away from the truth. The brother of confusion is chaos. With chaos and confusion working together, only the strong (true believers) will stand, because God shall be their cover.

Now you can see that people in the spiritual state of unconsciousness have their attention suspended. In other words, they don't see anything wrong in what they are doing, because they are locked in spiritually. Remember that the spiritual has more power than the physical. Being locked in spiritually by Satan and the powers of darkness, they themselves can't comprehend what they are doing in the first place or why. This is total wickedness, and the agenda of the devil and the powers of this world is that such people don't get saved, even after hours are spent trying to convert and teach them the truth. Please do not give up because not all hope is lost. I strongly encourage you as a child of the light (Jesus Christ) to keep trying and praying for these people. Pray that the power that has locked them into a spiritual sleeping state should release them in the name of Jesus Christ. Amen.

# ❦ 5 ❧

# *Causes of Spiritual Slumber*

¹ O foolish Galatians, who hath bewitched you, that ye should not obey the truth, before whose eyes Jesus Christ hath been evidently set forth, crucified among you?
² This only would I learn of you, Received ye the Spirit by the works of the law, or by the hearing of faith?
³ Are ye so foolish? having begun in the Spirit, are ye now made perfect by the flesh?
⁴ Have ye suffered so many things in vain? if it be yet in vain.
⁵ He therefore that ministereth to you the Spirit, and worketh miracles among you, doeth he it by the works of the law, or by the hearing of faith?
(Galatians 3:1–5 KJV)

I want you to say **"The SPRITUAL STATE OF THE HEART."**
The highway to spiritual sleep leads to resisting God's will

and purpose. Without doubt it propels its victims and leads to eternal condemnation (Matthew 7:13–14). The spiritual sleep and slumber highway is large (Isaiah 5:14) and has different levels, but they all end in one, which is death (Proverbs 14:12). Whichever level you find yourself on depends on the depth or level of your spiritual sleep.

As stated earlier, there are five stages in the cycle of natural sleep; similarly, the spiritual cycle also has five levels. In this regard, the level of spiritual slumbering is found in or represents the world of both unbelievers and believers. Stage one (beta-1 and beta-2) is found mostly among Christian believers who at one time may have been fully grounded in their walk with God. Some of these people were filled and led by the Holy Spirit. In the beta stage, as explained earlier, are people who may have gone out to evangelize and at that time would not compromise their faith. According to the terms of the Holy Bible, their love has become lukewarm or even grown cold.

The stage of spiritual sleep may deepen to loss of spiritual consciousness; an accompanying development is that one's fear and regard for God's word and commandments diminish. During the spiritual sleep state, the desire for the truth declines with an increasing depth to spiritual unconsciousness. This statement is not meant to be judgmental, but in truth there are believers in the church, but there is no Christ-consciousness in them.

It is sad to say that individuals in Spiritual Slumbering Stages four and five have become common in Christian gatherings. These people (SSS-4 and SSS-5) tend to use and see the gathering of God's children as a place to socialize. Jesus Christ went into the Temple at Jerusalem and threw away the money changers and flogged the people who were selling in the temple (Matthew

21:11–13). Similarly, the apostle Paul warned the church to be aware of people who are sent to deceive and cause confusion in the house of God (Romans 16:17–20).

Today, Christian gatherings have increased in number; this sometimes makes deceivers hard to identify, and there are many of such people among us. This is the reason why we strongly need sensitivity to the Holy Spirit to lead us and open our eyes as he had moved the apostle Peter in the case of Ananias and Sapphira (Acts 5:1–11) to be able to identify the wolf in sheep's clothing.

The root of spiritual sleep springs from the Garden of Eden (Genesis 3:1–19). In the Bible we read that the serpent told Eve that she would not die after eating the fruit which (she said) God had strictly instructed them not to even touch. Consequently, Satan did not tell Eve about the state of spiritual sleep, which he purposely omitted with the purpose of bringing forth disobedience.

Another important fact about the level of spiritual consciousness is that it does reflect the spiritual state of an individual's heart at a specific time. Remember that not all Christian are in these sleep stages as shown in Figure 1; most are not sleeping but are alert and awake. When Satan comes to tempt or lure anyone into a lesser state of consciousness, he will try to win their heart (trust) and gain their attention. This he also did to Eve, when she gave him her undivided attention in the Garden of Eden. For sin to come into and remain in a person who is a child of God, there must be a yielding and submission to that power. Yielding and submission criteria must be satisfied in the heart before anything can take place. If temptation starts from the heart, it is also right to say that sin starts from the heart.

In the Book of Genesis, God said to Cain before he killed

Abel, "sin is encroaching at your door; it desires to have you, but you must rule over it." (Genesis 4:7; 9-11 NIV). In 2 Samuel chapter 11 and 12, God asked King David through the mouth of the prophet Nathan a similar question about instructing him not to go into Bathsheba (12:9). Before getting involved in sin, there is a point when you will feel a resistance or hear a voice urging you to stop. What makes you listen or not listen to the voice of the Holy Spirit (or of Satan) depends on the spiritual state of your heart (consciousness).

Once led by the Holy Spirit to visit a place of worship, I was instructed to join the prayer team at that Church. While attending one of their weekly services one of the brothers in the prayer team asked me about "how can one tell their spiritual standing with God?" I answered him and said, "Your heart does tell you whether or not your standing is right with God or not." You can tell because the Holy Spirit will let you know. This why King David wrote, "Create in me a clean heart … and renew a right spirit within me. Cast me not away from thy presence" (Psalm 51:10–11). He wrote this because sin had come in to dwell in his heart, and the power of God had moved away. In such a case an individual with sense a quietness in respect to hearing from God.

The dwelling of the Holy Spirit is the place where he can communicate with your spirit-man, which can be found in your heart. When sin comes in to dwell in one's heart, the Holy Spirit moves away from the platform, and his voice becomes distant and faint (low). The level of the grieving the Holy Spirit can even windup in total detachment and silence (not hearing at all). I have often heard people refer the voice of the Holy Spirit to be a "still small voice." This information is taken from the Holy Bible, when the Lord asked the prophet Elijah to meet him in the mountain after he feared for his life and asked God to take him away (1 Kings 19:11-13). Remember, at first the voice was not still, nor was it small; rather, it was loud and focused in its agenda and purpose for the will of God. Fear can sometimes be considered as a sin. Fear holds people from yielding to the Holy Spirit, up to the point of even disobeying divine instructions. If sin is present and the person does not change or repent from that sin or transgression, the Holy Spirit will move further away but not totally away from the person. The consequence of this action is spiritual inaptness, which can lead to disconnection from the socket of the power of God and death.

As previously explained, there are five stages of spiritual sleep below that of a believer who is not in sin and walking in the light of God's will and power. The higher the stage number, the more completely the person is disconnected from the socket of God's power and deeper in spiritual sleep. Some people have given their lives to Christ but still live in sin. These people will quote the scripture even better than you can to them; yet the word of Christ they speak is not in them. This is why the Bible clearly states that it is not by acts of righteousness, but by faith alone that we can please God.

Going back to Figure 1, as previously noted, people in the alpha stage of spiritual sleep are those who find comfort under the umbrella of churchgoing and calling themselves Christians. These are called benchwarmers. Some of these people are wavering, undecided, and not sure if they want to commit themselves to the work of God. The alpha stage is well-known as the active stage of the sleep cycle. People in the alpha stage are very social in the church. The alpha group are those who are very spontaneous, as they can be in church on Sunday and be at a fetish priest chamber on Monday. These are people who consult palm readers and are interested in tarot-card and signs.

The third level, called the theta stage, represents those who believe in some form of powers or that God exists but continue to live their lives in a sinful way. These are people who will say they are theist in their beliefs but don't want to find out the truth. Some people in the theta stage will wave away the truth and tell you they are comfortable with their current spiritual state. These are people who put their trust in earthly riches and achievements and make decisions and judgments based on this ground or level.

The fourth level is called the fast delta stage of spiritual sleep. The fast delta waves characterizing this stage mean that these people are more resistant to God. These are people who may have heard about Jesus Christ but not in the context of giving their lives but as an opposition to their belief system. In this category are the people of the world (occultists, gangs, prostitutes, fetish priests, people of other religious backgrounds, and the people of the dark world). Most of these people have sold their souls or have taken oaths in the dark world and are classified as Anti-Christ.

The fifth level is the slow delta stage. These people sometimes call themselves atheists. They will verbally argue with you that there is no God. These are people who will try to use science to explain things that clearly demonstrate the existence of God. Some people in the slow delta stage grew up in a Christian home or a form of religious family but have made a conscious decision to go into a state of spiritual sleep or slumber. Their reasons for going into this state have been questioned, and their answers are often shaky. Some may blame it on their parents; some claim they felt tied down; others blame God for an unpleasant event that occurred in their life, and many more excuses. The truth is that these are all the intention of Satan and the power of darkness to prevent generational continuity in the pathway of faith and truth. This you will soon better understand as you read on.

"O foolish Galatians, who hath bewitched you, that ye should not obey the truth, before whose eyes Jesus Christ hath been evidently set forth, crucified among you?" (Galatians 3:1). You might phrase it this way: "O people, what has diverted your minds from the truth and caused you to fall asleep spiritually?" The Apostle Paul was perplexed by the people, as they were truly in a locked-in state and resisted the move of the power of God. The same behaviors are observed all around us, as you will come across people showing hatred toward anybody who talks to them about Jesus Christ. Every day these people wake up and never ask themselves questions about their existence and how everything in respect to their environment and the climate around them is happening. These people will insist that there is no God; some would rather seek help from palm readers (sorcerers and wizards) and fetish priests than be converted and commit to living a holy, righteous life in obedience to God's commandments.

Do not be perplexed about the recurrence of events regarding spirituality, because the demons of yesterday are the same ones working today. If the power of darkness seduced people and made the Israelites not to believe in the truth, they will do the same thing to people today and make them follow the pathway of deceit and lies, which lead to eternal condemnation and death.

Jesus said: "This people's heart is waxed gross, and their ears are dull of hearing, and their eyes they have closed" (Matthew 13:15). I want you to pay close attention to how Jesus Christ is describing the signs and symptoms associated with spiritual sleep and slumber. First, their heart is waxed gross, and the Holy Spirit and the Word of God can never dwell there. Second, their ears are dull of hearing and will not listen to the truth. Third, they have their eyes closed and have voluntarily (willingly) suspended their consciousness from seeing the truth and acknowledging their sinful nature. The sadness here is that they saw Jesus Christ performing miracles (sign and wonders), yet they did not believe in him or the power of God demonstrated before them. They would rather accuse Jesus Christ of using demonic powers to perform miracles (Matthews 12:23).

Do you ever wonder why spiritual Christians can still turn their backs on Christ and on the cross and sin again? It all starts from the heart, the eyes closed to the truth, and the ears closed to the call of the Holy Spirit. The heart state is what determines the desire to know God or to know the contrary. Therefore, sin is the epitome of spiritual sleep and slumber, and death is the outcome because the heart chooses it over good.

Sin start from the eye, to the heart, and then the mind. The mind is where the decision to act on a given directive, whether good or evil, takes place. The eye beholds, and it is the gateway to our soul, which is the "spiritual man." The spiritual man's headquarters is the heart. The heart is the platform of power and will. The heart (the spiritual mind) is the platform where spiritual battles and decisions are carried out. The heart is the place where the Holy Spirit communicates with your spiritual man. Whatever is decided in the heart, the natural mind (which includes the brain and body) will carry it out. This is why subjecting your body in its totality to the power of God can give you the strength to resist sin—even when the heart has agreed to do otherwise.

# Consequences of Your Actions

The Bible states clearly that "the wages of sin is death; but the gift of God is eternal life through Jesus Christ our Lord" (Romans 6:23). Satan (the devil) and the powers of darkness are fully aware that anything that goes contrary to the Word of God brings death. Furthermore, sin, disobedience, transgression, and trespasses are spiritual fertilizer to the breeding ground where demonic powers operate and thrive. For the same reason Satan (also called Lucifer) thought to destroy humanity in the Garden of Eden, because he understood that the consequence of disobeying God's instructions is death. Thank God that little did he know that it was just spiritual death. God in his infinite wisdom, did not want us his creation to be destroyed; rather, he issued a judgment against humankind (his creation) and Satan, as noted in Genesis 3:14–19.

The consequence of Adam and Eve's disobedience in the Garden of Eden on everyone born to a woman is spiritual death—with a consequence if the person does not repent: eternity in the wrath of God. Aware or unaware, those who do not repent while they pass through this earth, if they die in sin, consequently will spend eternity in the wrath of God (eternal lake of fire) to come when Jesus Christ returns to judge the world. I have often heard people mistake hell itself for the lake of fire. These are two different places. In the Day of Judgment, death and hell will also be judged and cast into the lake of fire (Revelation 20:14). Hell is before the pre-rapture return of Jesus Christ, and the lake of fire is for the Judgment Day—simply put, double punishment for the wicked and disobedient.

We all have in us the willpower and the spirit of the old man (the body of disobedience and power of sin). The potential and propensity to disobey God's word is in everybody born by a woman; the devil knows this very well. Since we are all born naturally into sin, after repenting and accepting Jesus Christ, we all can be seduced and lured into sin against God's word and commandments; against Jesus Christ who died for our sins; and against the Holy Spirit. Only allowing Satan to deceive you, and your willing response to that impulse to sin, enables you to go against the will of God.

When born-again believers sin, such an act is inflicted on the body, which is the temple of God. This is something that every child of God should know and remember, that for the devil to reduce or remove the power of the Holy Spirit, sin must come in to dwell. The devil will do anything to pollute your temple (the indwelling of God's power to resist sin). The consequence of sin, trespasses, and transgression is spiritual detachment from God's power socket and the vessel's sinking into a state of spiritual slumber or sleep. Consequently, people snared in this way soon start to get comfortable with sin and may further resist God's words if they don't repent.

I have met Christian believers who said to me things that compelled me to confront them with questions about their state of Christ consciousness and their standing with God. You will hear these people saying things like "You are too strict (no fun) and too rigid"; "You pray too much, and you are disturbing God with your praying"; and some will advise you to "please enjoy yourself, and don't kill yourself for the sake of the gospel." Some believers will say, "There are other Christians doing it, so why can't I do it?" I have also heard people say, "I will never forget it, and I will never forgive; I hate that brother/sister." These are signs and symptoms of spiritual immaturity, and discernment reveals these believers as "unbroken or unyielded" to the power of the Holy Spirit.

Another scale to assess or categorize a person's stage of spiritual slumbering is their comfort with using profanity and curse words; stealing (or taking part in it); gossiping; and telling lies. The Bible warns us as believers that we are not to allow corrupt words—or anything that does not edify others spiritually or glorify our God in heaven—to proceed out from our mouth (see Ephesians 4:29–30). Jesus proclaimed to the multitude, and said unto them, "Hear, and understand: Not that which goeth into the mouth defileth a man; but that which cometh out of the mouth, this defileth a man" (Matthew 15:10–11). We are children of God Most High, and believers and unbelievers alike are held accountable for everything we say as long as we remain on this Earth. If we are all accountable for our actions and words, as believers, we must demonstrate spiritual maturity and mastery of our emotions and senses.

## The Plantings of Righteousness

If the Bible does mention and speak about seed of the light and seeds of righteousness, there must also be seeds of darkness and seeds unrighteousness, which are not of God. The fruits and seeds a person bears or produces are the product of their spiritual state of consciousness. Before moving further to discuss the importance of spiritual seeds and their attributes, let us draw a clear understanding of what a seed is.

As most of us know, a seed is the smallest part of a plant; yet it contains the potential for producing the next generation of that specific plant. The seed contains the genetic code; whenever that code is activated, it will yield both a new tree and eventually fruits like those of the mother tree. With respect to good and evil, there is the seed of light, which of God, and the seed of darkness, which is of the devil. Encrypted with the seed of light is the word of God, and those who receive the word of truth in their lives are transformed into spiritual trees. In the spiritual realm, the supernatural power of transformation comes from God or Satan, and it can work only on those who yield their totality to do either good or evil.

Every seed is created naturally uncorrupted, but it becomes corrupted from the womb because of sin. Just as a virus will implant itself on a host cell to dictate and redirect the host's function, so also sin has power over the natural body. In addition, the power to change from a tree of good to evil, and vice versa, is activated only based on conscious decisions and will go either way. In other words, you cannot be both a good and evil tree at the same time, just as no tree in our world is both an apple tree and at the same time an orange tree. Finally, the power for transformation is the Word of God, which is the antidote that can do away with the power of Satan.

When a seed is transformed, it is planted in the vineyard of God, where it is nourished to grow. Upon maturity, each tree will produce fruits and seeds based on the encrypted power of the gene it possesses. Within each fruit are seeds that can be replanted. As a planting of the Lord, the seeds you are expected to produce are seeds of righteousness, which are the products of your godly acts and your belief in Jesus Christ. The fruits you bear are the product of both internal and external forces working upon you, with the sole purpose for you to be fruitful.

If the seed of light is the Word of God, and the Word of God is Jesus Christ (John 1:1–3), then the seeds you produce within your fruits are seeds of righteousness. In addition, all you need is a single sowing of the spiritual seed (the Word of God) to be transformed into a tree. When the seed is put into the soil, according to Jesus Christ, it must first die, lest it abides alone; its purpose is to die and produce fruit (John 12:24). In other words, for the power of God to fully take possession of that seed and take it into the next level, which is the level of transformation, it must die to itself. When a natural seed dies to itself (physical nature), it starts to undergo many biophysiochemical processes that can only take place by its yielding to the forces of nature and principles (ordinances) put in place by God (Genesis 1:29). Similarly, the spiritual seed must also die and yield itself totally for the forces of the supernatural power to take it to the next level of spiritual transformation. It behooves us to yield our totality to Christ Jesus to experience the true power of God and live. The spiritual seed dies, and through the power of God it lives to become a tree of righteousness, planted in the vineyard of God's house. The seed is dead and has now become a tree rooted in the power of God's will and is no longer abiding alone. The tree of righteousness will be moved neither by the physical forces of nature nor by the forces of darkness but rather by the spiritual force rooted in Jesus Christ.

The supernatural power for the survival, nourishment, and viability of the spiritual tree comes from the Holy Spirit and the word of God (Jesus Christ). The Word of God states that we are the planting of the Lord (Isaiah 61:3), and as a planting, we are expected to grow by harnessing nutriments provided by God. Continuous nourishment is needed to go into the next level, which is the stage of spiritual maturity. The next level, upon achieving spiritual maturity, is the bringing forth of spiritual fruits.

In the natural world, the fruits that a tree produces depend on the type of tree, as stated earlier. A tree will only produce its kind and not another. Furthermore, according to the word of God, you are the tree of the Lord, and you are expected to bear fruits of holiness and righteousness, to the honor and glory of your Father in heaven. Within the fruit is the seed. The fruits of righteousness are products of God's power working inside you physically and spiritually, and its manifestations are attributable to holiness and perfection, which replicates the blueprint of the nature of God. The contrary takes place when a plant is corrupted. The product of such a plant is the fruits of corruption, which possess within them the seed of sin and disobedience.

The fruit you bear is a product of the power that is working within you; hence, the Holy Bible encourages us to avoid anything that does not glorify our Father in heaven or that goes against his commandment; therein lie seeds of darkness (Matthew 7:16–20). Every tree that is corrupted and those trees that do not bear fruit will be destroyed by the Lord and cast into the fire for destruction.

> **Finally, brethren, whatsoever things are true, whatsoever things are honest, whatsoever things are just, whatsoever things are pure, whatsoever things are lovely, whatsoever things are of good report; if there be virtue, and if there be any praise, think on these things. Those things, which ye have both learned, and received, and heard, and seen in me, do: and the God of peace shall be with you. (Philippians 4:8–9)**

In Philippians 4:8, the Apostle Paul starts with the word *finally*, to indicate that he sums up his exhortation this way: that whatsoever things are pure, lovely, of good report, and spiritually edifying, those are where you need to stay focused. In verse 9, Apostle Paul encourages believers to follow godly principles. His agenda for writing those letter to the churches, as instructed by our Lord Jesus Christ, was to encourage and admonish believers- at that time and us currently—that those things we have received and heard through the word of God, those things that are associated with the body of Christ, those things we have seen other followers who truly fear their God do—we are expected to perpetuate them in our daily life.

As a planting of righteousness, which makes you a child and a part and parcel of God's will, you must act so as not to diminish or delay the true nature of the power of Jesus Christ, the light of God. Engaging in acts that do not edify you in the things of God takes you slowly or quickly into deeper levels of spiritual sleep or slumber, which is a low state of spiritual consciousness. As stated earlier, the consequence of walking in a low state of consciousness is that one dwells in a low spiritual energy state of inattentiveness. Inattentive people are not conscious of things going on around them, unless their attention is drawn to them. The only way you can be truly attentive is when you have the Holy Spirit, which helps you focus your attention on the Light, which is Jesus Christ. I encourage you today to surrender your whole body and willpower totally to the doing of God's will, and he will give you peace from all sides. Isaiah 26:3, addressing the Lord, affirms, "Thou wilt keep him in perfect peace, whose mind is stayed on thee: because he trusteth in thee."

This is not to scare you, but to give you the truth. There is a form of spiritual sleep or slumber that is associated with people utilizing demonic powers to spiritually manipulate people or blind their victims. Demonic powers and enchantments are commonly in use now, especially in the corporate world where people who are educated indulge in such acts to gain success, wealth, and favor. These people themselves are at the theta stage through delta stage of spiritual slumber. They are in the theta stage because they believe in some form of power which they themselves are using; they are in the delta stage because they are hiding their true nature, so their victims can relax while they are working behind closed doors. These people utilize demonic powers to manipulate their victims to do whatever they desire.

This was the same reason King Nebuchadnezzar of Babylon stood at a crossroads and consulted omens before engaging his enemies to defeat in battle (Ezekiel 21:21). This is the reason why the children of God must pray daily and meditate on God's word. Give yourself to godly acts, and keep yourself pure—away from sin. When demonic spirits see you as a person, they can tell your spiritual state as either awake or asleep (Mark 3:11; Luke 8:28). Those who are spiritually awake and alert will always stand out as conquerors; they can never be oppressed because they bear within them the fruit of the light (the power of God). When darkness encounters the light, the darkness is totally terminated as if it never existed: "And the light shineth in darkness; and the darkness comprehended it not" (John 1:5).

## The Mark of Jesus Christ I Bear

Another thing that differentiates the seed of light from the seed of darkness is the mark of Jesus Christ, which we all bear as his disciples. "And as many as walk according to this rule, peace be on them, and mercy, and upon the Israel of God. From henceforth let no man trouble me: for I bear in my body the marks of the Lord Jesus" (Galatians 6:16–17). The mark of Jesus Christ is the symbol of his coming to Earth in human form, walking on this earth without sin, his crucifixion on the cross of Calvary, his resurrection from the dead, and his ascending into heaven. The mark of Jesus Christ is the manifestation of God's power, which now lives and works in us who believe in him and walk in his light.

Henceforth let nobody trouble me, for I bear in my body the mark of Christ. The mark of Christ you bear is your identity as a believer. Your belief in Jesus Christ and his word working in you are accounted for as your faith and trust in him.

Your faith is your spiritual muscle, which can become enlarged based on how much of the word of the Lord you possess. Bodybuilder build their muscles through continuous exercising their muscle. Similarly, continuous exercising in the spiritual perspective also enlarges your faith. Faith is also the size and sharpness of your spiritual sword, and not a spiritual currency, because you are not gambling with Satan. Faith also refers to a believer's spiritual strength, because it is the power of God that makes you strong. Hence there is power and there is a power that can never be contended with. The Holy Bible clearly states that, first, the weapons of our warfare are not carnal but mighty through God to the pulling down of every stronghold (2 Corinthians 10:4). Second, we wrestle not against flesh and blood, but against spiritual powers (Ephesians 6:12). Third, we walk by faith and not by sight (2 Corinthians 5:7). Faith is believing and putting your hope on things that are not seen (Hebrews 11:1). What made you believe in those things not seen is the seed of light that was sown into your life and has transformed you into a tree of righteousness and holiness.

Faith is a verb, just as is sleep. A verb is a word used to describe an action, state, or occurrence, and forming the main part of the predicate of a sentence (Dictionary.com). Faith is an acting out or a reflection of your spiritual state of mind. Faith is the belief component arising from the power of conviction, which is bestowed upon you—through the Word of God—with an intent of achieving a desired outcome. The outcome of faith can be either positive or negative. Faith is positive when it aligns with the word and will of God. Faith is negative when it is contrary to the will and word of God. Faith is not your spiritual currency in heaven, but righteousness is the spiritual currency. Faith is your belief or mind-set at a given time, while your righteousness is what grants you access into heaven; as it also determines how and where you will be living in heaven. Faith becomes effective when your attitude is showing trust (James chapters 1–3). Jesus Christ clearly declared to the people that unless their righteousness exceeded that of the Pharisees, they would not enter the Kingdom of Heaven (see Matthew 5:20).

Righteousness is measured, and faith is the state of the heart. Faith comes by hearing and hearing by the word of God. The Word of God you hear works inside you and transforms you to bring out the true fruits of righteousness. Then faith (the word of God) is your sword and shield, and righteousness is your breastplate (which bears your rank and identity). In the physical realm identity is very important; so also in the spiritual realm. Your identity reflects your standing with God. Your standing reflects on both your faith (because without faith you can't please God) and righteousness (without which you can't get into heaven). The only thing that can take away a true child of

God's identity is sin and a conscious decision to totally reject Jesus Christ (transgression).

To transgress means to go against God's law or commandment with complete rejection and resistance to the voice of the Holy Spirit. Transgression is associated with a person having full knowledge about what is wrong and what is right; however, with this knowledge the person still makes a conscious decision to do what is wrong against the word of God. It is sad to see many believers turning their back on Jesus Christ and their God. There is no loss that can be compared to the loss of your soul. There is no amount of wealth, fame, position, pleasure, or gain that is worth your soul. Salvation is free, and your soul is priceless. Giving away your soul for earthly things that perish, or for things that we die and leave behind, is worthless. If you are contemplating or have gone against God's word and commandments, I encourage you to come back to the Lord and ask for forgiveness.

> **Yea, doubtless, and I count all things but loss for the excellency of the knowledge of Christ Jesus my Lord: for whom I have suffered the loss of all things, and do count them but dung, that I may win Christ, and be found in him, not having mine own righteousness, which is of the law, but that which is through the faith of Christ, the righteousness which is of God by faith: that I may know him, and the power of his resurrection, and the fellowship of his sufferings, being made conformable unto his death. (Philippians 3:8–10)**

The apostle Paul here states clearly that nothing can be compared to the gain of receiving Jesus Christ into his life; furthermore, that those things the world exalts as high and important are nothing but a waste and can never be compared to the gain of righteousness realized through faith in God and salvation itself through Christ Jesus, our Lord and Savior. Therefore, anything that holds you back from fully yielding yourself to Jesus Christ is nothing but a waste (dung) and can never supersede the excellence of the knowledge and power of God. Conviction and appreciation for the power of God come from embracing God's gift of salvation to humanity through his Son, Jesus Christ.

To be transformed by the power of God through his word, you must open yourself to the truth. Salvation is truly free, but for you to experience the gift and benefits of salvation, you must make a genuine decision to change for good in your heart. Just as in a marriage or relationship, when the heart is not fully involved or appreciative of what it has been offered, it becomes disgruntled. This is the reason many people fall away from the way of truth. When the consciousness is not fully appreciated, people start to seek after spiritual sleep and slumber to resolve issues of life.

The power most often behind this falling away is Satan using seducing words to lure people away. I have been a victim of the luring, and thank God that I was shaken back from sleep, thanks to people who were praying for me, including my lovely mother. Satan will make you feel that people of the world are having more fun and are happier than you as a believer. Satan will tell you that remaining in the pathway of truth is a waste of time and that you need to go out and mingle with unrighteousness. Satan will tell you that nobody can be righteous and holy as God. Satan and the power of darkness will use all these lies and many more to try to convince you to turn away. In order to stand your ground through faith, you must have your heart and mind stayed (steady) on the word of truth. What does the word of truth teach us? The word of truth teaches us to hate evil with all our heart and soul, as well as anything that opposes (is contrary to) holiness and righteousness.

## ∼ 6 ∼

# What Happens When You Are Spiritually Asleep?

**²⁵ But while men slept, his enemy came and sowed tares among the wheat, and went his way. ²⁶ But when the blade was sprung up, and brought forth fruit, then appeared the tares also. ²⁷ So the servants of the householder came and said unto him, Sir, didst not thou sow good seed in thy field? from whence then hath it tares? ²⁸ He said unto them, An enemy hath done this. The servants said unto him, Wilt thou then that we go and gather them up? (Matthew 13:25-28 KJV)**

When you live a life of spiritual sleep and slumber, you stand to lose a lot. Spiritual sleep and slumber open you to spiritual attacks, failures, sadness, depression, a feeling of incompleteness, and despair. Other characteristics linked to the state of spiritual sleep and slumber are prayerlessness, little to no time spent in the Lord's presence, and a complete loss of interest in meditating on God's word. Spiritual sleep and slumbering periods also open a Christian or full believer to demonization, spiritual pollution, and perversion.

This does not mean that if a day goes by when you don't read your Bible or pray, things will always go wrong; however, whether good or bad things take place depends on your sensitivity to the Holy Spirit at that period. The longer you abstain from prayer and meditation, the spiritually weaker you become. When you are weak spiritually, the power to resist temptation is low. Hence, you may come across Christians who feel comfortable going to night clubs and getting involved in fornication and adultery without a pennyworth of guilt that they have done something wrong. Some may even fall into the sin of telling a lie when they themselves question the motive behind the lies. This is the power of Satan, whose intention is to stain your white garment with smears of ungodliness.

If the statement above describes you or reflects your spiritual condition, you are in a state of spiritual sleep and slumber. If you are a believer held at a higher level to be a responsible leader in the faith, but you are still watching pornography, masturbating, or spending time engaging in inappropriate affairs with a believer or unbeliever, you are in a state of spiritual sleep and slumber. In addition, you are subjecting yourself intentionally to a lesser state of consciousness. Whenever you engage yourself in talking and enacting hatred, stereotypes, and racism, you are spiritually asleep and a murderer (1 John 3:15). Just as natural sleep creeps up on it victim, so also spiritual sleep and slumber can come in and take control of one's senses. There have been several occasions where members or workers in the church have been caught doing things that they should not be doing, even in the house of God. Please, whenever you come across such people, pass to them this message: "God wants you to arise from that spiritual sleep and slumber." *Wake up in the name of Jesus Christ!*

## $\mathcal{C}$onscience and Consciousness

These two words *conscience* and *consciousness* are sometime misused because they are both pointing in the direction of the mind state, but they have two separate meanings. Consciousness and conscience can be used together implicitly to describe the extent to which an individual has lost touch with their true nature.

No person is born to be evil, although we are born into sin. This is a clearly stated fact in the Holy Scripture that anyone conceived and given birth to by a woman is born into a corrupt nature, which is the flesh. As the born child grows, the child soon learns the power of making choices. This is especially encountered in the age when little toddlers say *"No"* to everything except their favorite snacks and milk. Children also learn to differentiate things, as well as impose their desires and needs on their caregiver.

The ability to make choices is called free will. As a parent you will be surprised when a child reacts in a certain way when caught doing something wrong, despite being young and tender minded. Do not be alarmed, because the nature and power of God are working in each and every one of us.

Whether we like it or not, we are created in the image and likeness of God. According to Genesis, the serpent told Eve in the Garden of Eden that consumption of the forbidden fruit would awaken the power of knowledge between good and evil. The power of knowledge to differentiate between good and evil came for disobedience through lies and seductions. God never wanted people to be put into a situation where they must choose between good and evil and between life and death. The child's reaction comes from the power that was working in that child while it was still developing in the womb.

As parents we are to teach and train our children to do good, even utilizing expiating methodology. As a child's brain continues to develop, the power for physical consciousness begins to increase, but it is not concrete to fully understand the consequence of their actions whether it be good or evil. Just like a baby that bits you and smiles after doing it. That child is not smiling because he/she is a sadist who like to inflate pain in others. The child laughs because you flinched and screamed for pain, and this expression amuses the child because the consciousness of still developing. Children at the beginning stages of their lives may even see angels and other spirits. Many parents have one time or another stumbled on their toddlers stirring or smiling back at something an observing adult can't see. This stage of the toddler's life is called the spiritual eye-opening-experience. The spiritual eye-opening-experience is a way that God uses to test the spiritual senses to make sure they are working. The spiritual senses are disconnected and usually stop when toddlers can actually speak and fully express themselves with words. A good example to show that the Spiritual senses is activated before the natural, is the blind man that Jesus restored his eyes. The first thing the man saw were the spiritual world (men as tall as trees), before Jesus Christ touched the eyes again for the natural to be restored (Mark 8:24-25). In the perspective of the young growing mind, some children may continue to encounter these spirits and angels, depending on their destiny and assignment on Earth. These encounters may also continue as dreams; however, as parents we must continue to pray over our children and anoint them before they go to bed in the name of our Lord and Savior, Jesus Christ.

As children develop, their physical consciousness is increased, which is contingent on their physical senses. Children to some degree are not as alert or aware as an adult, since consciousness functions in the context of awareness. What can be extrapolated from what has been discussed so far is that conscience is innate, while consciousness is acquired with time. For this reason, a child will demonstrate either love and kindness or else hatred and unkindness, not fully aware of the consequence or effect of their action on others.

As children continue to grow, they soon learn what is called projection and reflection. Projection (or abstract thinking) is the ability to use the brain to strategize or plan a reciprocal response from a subject. When children display this behavior, using their mind to influence the behavior of their parents, an observer is put in awe. A good example is seen daily at the supermarkets, when a child begins to cry intensely when they want their parent to succumb to their demand for candy or toys displayed on the shelves. Parents often ask their child, "Where did you learn that?" The power of knowledge of good and evil is the power of will and conscience. The willpower and conscience can be exercised to do good or evil because it is based on individual decision. God will never impose on your willpower. However, the home base for willpower and conscience is located within the heart. For this reason, if you can manipulate the conscience, you can indirectly control the willpower.

When consciousness has fully developed, your conscience, which is innate, will quickly impose itself and dictate its operations. Just when the conscience starts to dictate for the consciousness varies among people; that is why it is easy to change a bad child through persuasion to become good. No matter how good the consciousness may be, when the conscience is good, it will cause the consciousness to be aligned with good and repel evil. On the other hand, when the conscience is deadened and full of evil, the consciousness will be evil. Do you ever wonder why serial killers, scammers, rapists, and people who revel in perpetrating wickedness never feel remorse? Now you know: their conscience and willpower have been programed to do evil.

Satan and the power of darkness do manipulate the consciousness and conscience; however, they can never manipulate your free will. Free will is the ability to choose the direction of knowledge to follow. Remember the road for knowledge is split into two, and the choice of which way to go depends on you. Conscience and consciousness are where the Holy Spirit can also work on a person but not on their willpower. The willpower is untouchable; hence, God will work with you only at the level of conscience and consciousness. Hebrews 9:14 states that the blood of Jesus will cleanse your conscience. The scripture also states that we "overcame [Satan] by the blood of the Lamb [Jesus Christ], and by the word of [our] testimony"; but our free will God does not interfere with or impose his power on.

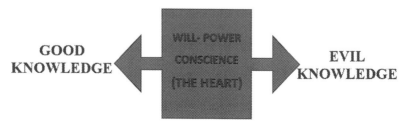

FIGURE: 2: THE PATHWAY OF WILL POWER,
CONSCIENCE & KNOWLEDGE

The blood of Jesus Christ works at the level of conscience and consciousness. The blood of Jesus Christ cleanses your conscience when you submit your willpower to his will and power. The blood of Jesus Christ cleanses your conscience when you allow the light of God to come into your life, as the power in his blood cleanses and purges you from all your sins (1 John 1:7). If you without doubting submit your willpower totally to Jesus Christ, the power of the light will revive you, and your spiritual man will be awakened from spiritual sleep and slumber. As a result, you will start to hate evil and seek after holiness and righteousness, which is the power of God working in his light.

When the contrary takes place and one does not surrender their totality (body [mind], soul [heart] and spirit), even just partially submission, their spiritual consciousness and conscience will not be regenerated (awakened). As spiritual sleep intensifies, the consciousness and conscience are diminished; this is when even a believer's faith may be compromised with ease. Then one's resistance to what is unholy wanes away. This is the dilemma of believers because their faith can be challenged at each moment of their lives. These testing of your faith comes in many forms and situations. You may also encounter opposition in situations of whenever you try to speak the truth, you will meet people whose beliefs have been either compromised or uncompromised or even absent.

The number of those who have compromised is increasing daily because this is what the Lord spoke about that will all take place in the last days. In the pretribulation era, people will do everything to be accepted within a certain group. The desire to be accepted is where a lot of people will experience a downfall, because it can result in making the wrong choices in life.

It is true that no one has full power to will the compass of their destiny; but you as an individual do have the willpower to direct your faith towards a specific direction. There are some individuals who choose not to make choices and instead go with the flow and remain in neutral, uncommitted. This state of mind displeases the Lord, because it is nothing else but falsehood. God hates for anyone called into the light to be in this state of slumber and falsehood. It is a state of falsehood because the person is trying to play mind games on both other people and God.

In the faith it is better to be at either end than to be in the middle. In other words, if you are a Christian, then be a Christian. Be bold and take your stance in the faith, as a lot of people hate making choices, especially in the matter of faith. The gospel truth is that you must make a choice. You must make a choice to belong to God or to belong to the devil. Satan knows that people love the middle or neutral position where (they think) they are not confronted or held to be responsible. This is the deception about not making a choice; yet their actions are making it for them based on their spiritual state of consciousness.

When you are an unbelieving Christian or unbeliever, you automatically go into a state of spiritual Slumber. At the other extreme of the spectrum which is being a true believer; when you are a believer of Christ Jesus, you die to the natural-consciousness and be awakened spiritually in holiness, truth and righteousness (spiritual-consciousness).

## $\mathcal{H}$ard to Hear from God.

Spiritual sleep or slumber makes it hard to hear from God and the Holy Spirit. The church is suffering from spiritual scarcity in respect to hearing from God. Looking back at the time of the prophets Samuel, Elijah, and Elisha and the judges Gideon and Samson, the Bible mentions that it was then rare for people to hear from God, even though there were many prophets and prophetesses in the whole of Israel and Judah. Even before the time of Jesus Christ's ministry on Earth began, there was scarcity in hearing from God.

This spiritual deafness came as a repercussion because of disobedience and the fact that sin increased, and the Spirit of God fell silent. When sin abounds the power of the lower state of spiritual consciousness sets in, and the Spirit of God gets quiet and moves to the side. The truth is that God never moves away; rather, the Holy Spirit, which is the Voice of God, gets quiet. Remember that the platform for your spiritual microphone is in your heart. The Holy Spirit moving away from your spiritual microphone makes it hard to hear from God and hard to obey.

In Jeremiah 42 we read how the people of Judah, after the invasion of Jerusalem by King Nebuchadnezzar, went to the prophet Jeremiah and asked him to pray for them to God. They asked the prophet because they knew that God would not answer them if they tried to pray. The power of sin and disobedience closes the ears and makes it hard to hear from God. The power of sin and disobedience, if not addressed appropriately, makes the prayer of the sinner stink before God.

King Solomon wrote: "Dead flies makes the oil of the perfumer give off a foul odor; so a little foolishness [in one who is esteemed] outweighs wisdom and honor (Ecclesiastes 10:1 AMP.)." The perfumer ointment is supposed to have a sweet perfume smell, but because it has been contaminated by the flies, it starts to stink. So also is prayer coming from an unrepentant sinner before God. Simply said: "Sin makes your prayer unacceptable to God." For this reason, Jesus Christ came to make it possible for us to come into the presence of God to ask for forgiveness. You must repent of your sin first before requesting help from God. You can never outsmart God, who searches the heart and intents of everyone.

## $\mathcal{R}$uling Power on Your Tower

The Bible clearly warns us to guard our heart "with all diligence; for out of it are the issues of life" (Proverbs 4:23). When the heart steps into sin and the temple of God (your body) is defiled, the Holy Spirit moves away from the platform (tower) where the spiritual microphone is located, and he becomes hard to hear and obey. Hence the words *still* and *small* pertaining to his voice. Obeying God's instructions becomes difficult and a burden because the things that are holy don't sit well with the flesh that is not fully crucified.

The apostle Paul in the Bible states: "I die daily" and "I now live" (1 Corinthians 15:31; Galatians 2:20). I die to sin (spiritual sleep and slumber) daily because I open myself consciously to the power of the Holy Spirit (a higher level of spiritual consciousness) and to the promises of God power (Jesus Christ). Therefore, because of this action, the life that I live now I live by faith; old things have passed away, and now I live in Jesus Christ, my Lord and Savior, who died for me.

Many Christian believers are unaware of their spiritual state and may or may not be concerned about it. The question is "What happens when you are spiritually asleep?" As a spiritual sleeping and slumbering child of God, there is a great tendency for you to find yourself in a vicious circle of hatred, racism, and being biased, stereotypic, and always negative and judgmental against other people, covetous, greedy, and gossiping.

Gossip is a big issue in the church and needs to be taken

seriously and addressed. The Bible uses the word *slanderer* to describe a gossip. It is clearly stated in the Bible that all gossips will be among those that shall be cast into the lake of fire. If you find yourself in such a situation, as a fellow worker in the body of Christ, I encourage you to ask the Holy Spirit to help you control your tongue and emotion. It is not worth a thing that your tongue and emotion should lead you away from God's promise (Hebrews 4:1).

> Mortify therefore your members which are upon the earth; fornication, uncleanness, inordinate affection, evil concupiscence, and covetousness, which is idolatry: for which things' sake the wrath of God cometh on the children of disobedience: in the which ye also walked some time, when ye lived in them.
>
> But now ye also put off all these; anger, wrath, malice, blasphemy, filthy communication out of your mouth. Lie not one to another, seeing that ye have put off the old man with his deeds; and have put on the new man, which is renewed in knowledge after the image of him that created him. (Colossians 3:5–10)

The Word of God clearly states that we are to stay away from anything that defiles the temple of God. It is our duty as the children of God who are enlightened in his Word to endeavor to follow what Jesus Christ represents. We are never to engage in sin or anything that may look innocent but leads to hell and eternal condemnation. The word that the Lord wants me to tell you here is that every believer should be *awake* and *paying attention* through prayers and meditation on his Word; hence comes the instruction to "Watch and pray" (Matthew 26:41). You can only watch and pray when you are spiritually alert and awake. For this reason, Satan will try to stop you from surrendering yourself to the power of the Holy Spirit or spending time in the presence of God. The only way to keep your heart clean and ready for God is through praying, meditating on God's Word, and fasting. The power to control and resist sin comes entirely from your totally yielding to the Holy Spirit. When you are filled with the Holy Spirit, his voice is no longer still and quiet but loud and clear.

Galatians 5:13 says: "For, brethren, ye have been called unto liberty; only use not liberty for an occasion to the flesh, but by love serve one another." Verse 16 says: "This I say then, Walk in the Spirit, and ye shall not fulfil the lust of the flesh." Verse 26 says: "Let us not be desirous of vain glory, provoking one another, envying one another." Verse 14 reminds us: "Thou shalt love thy neighbor as thyself." The word of God clearly states that even though we are born again and Spirit-filled and operating in the power of God, we should never use this as a reason or an advantage for ourselves to do wrong to others around us. In other words, in our spiritual walk with God, we should portray Christ (holiness and righteousness) in whatever we do and walk in love. Paul offers his own imitation of Christ as a model:

> **For our exhortation was not of deceit, nor of uncleanness, nor in guile: but as we were allowed of God to be put in trust with the gospel, even so we speak; not as pleasing**

**men, but God, which trieth our hearts. For neither at any time used we flattering words, as ye know, nor a cloke of covetousness; God is witness. (1 Thessalonians 2:3–5)**

The Holy Spirit through the Apostle Paul's letter here strictly warns us not to work the works of darkness (deceit -seeds of Satan) but to display righteousness, faith, love, honesty, integrity, and truth (Seeds of God). The desire of God is to see everybody—if possible—walking in the liberty with Jesus Christ that we obtained through his death on the cross, growing in his light, and bringing forth uncorrupted fruits. In addition, Gods' desire is to see that, as true believers called into his grace, we become awakened spiritually and able to resist temptations, sin, and Satan, through subjecting our body to obey and grow in his power. I will stress this again and again: *The power of God becomes stronger when we engage in Bible reading, meditation, and worshipping God in our homes and wherever we can, in song of praises and psalms.*

## When They Sleep

Matthew 13:25 states: "But while men slept, his enemy came and sowed tares among the wheat, and went his way." If you are spiritually awake, the enemy will not step into your life any way they like, because they know you will destroy them. Those in spiritual sleep and slumber cannot tell when the enemy came, what the enemy did, or what was stolen, damaged, or dumped into their life, because the power of wakefulness is unavailable (Jeremiah 17:6). Their eyes are open, yet they are unable to see because they are spiritually blind (unconscious and/or unaware) and have set their mind to resist the truth.

These people are spiritually inept; they are only depending on natural senses and impulses to help them, which clearly will not be able to save them. *Inept* is a word used here to refer to a state of spiritual inactivity, incompetence, and dysfunctional. In a spiritual state of ineptness, God in his infinite love and mercy does not leave you alone, but still guides you. The guidance you get is based on what you are relying on as your guide. This is true because when you come across a totally blind person, they tend to channel their senses to other parts of their body as point of reference and for guidance.

Another issue with spiritual sleep or slumber is being out of touch with reality. Deception is going on around us and lures people away from the truth. Life is a complicated place, but without complications at times, people will not venture out in search of the truth. Without complications and hardship, people will not seek God, and this is seen even among the rich. Most rich people put their confidence in their wealth to save them and not in God. This mentality or way of thinking displeases the Lord; but the world is teaching and instilling this doctrine.

This doctrine and belief in wealth is taught so often that there are several conferences held on how to become rich; but those teaching how to live a holy life on earth are few. Revelation 3:15–17 says:

> I know thy works, that thou art neither cold
> nor hot: I would thou wert cold or hot. So then
> because thou art lukewarm, and neither cold nor
> hot, I will spue thee out of my mouth. Because
> thou sayest, I am rich, and increased with goods,

and have need of nothing; and knowest not that
thou art wretched, and miserable, and poor, and
blind, and naked.

Putting trust in flesh and blood and in earthly riches is the delusion that leads to destruction. There is nothing wrong with being rich, because King Solomon was a child of God and was the richest man in the world. King Solomon wrote in Ecclesiastes 10:19 that "money answereth all things" and does create avenue for growth; however, it can also lead to destruction. The deception that money creates an atmosphere of joy has backfired, as we read about millionaires feeling lonely and empty. These people gave their all and did attain the optimum heights for worldly achievements and wealth; however, when the reality (of being miserable, poor, blind, and naked) has set in; and today these individuals they no more. God consider such people who forsake him as wicked, as the wealth that they gather will be given away to people who did not labor for it (Proverbs 13:22 & Ecclesiastes 2:26)

On the same side of the spectrum of deception is what happens among our youth. In our world today, the youth and their parents are focused on getting into sports and getting drafted; but most of these children have not thought to put God first. A young man or woman must be shown and taught that nothing else in this world should take a higher place than God. It is God who gives wealth and opportunities for promotions, not your skills or talent. When you put God first, he will make you rise above your competitors, and the wealth that you gather will stay with you even forever. This is the downfall of many who are following the pathway of not honoring or placing their trust in the Lord.

My young and talented individual, I want you to know that the world and everything within it all belongs to God; including the wealth of this world. So therefore, set not your heart on these things because they are temporary and perish. Revelation 3:18 says: **"I counsel thee to buy of me gold tried in the fire, that thou mayest be rich; and white raiment, that thou mayest be clothed, and that the shame of thy nakedness do not appear; and anoint thine eyes with eyesalve, that thou mayest see."**

You are to fix your eyes on Jesus Christ, because he is the author and finisher of your faith. When you pray and follow after holiness and righteousness, those loopholes that Satan has crafted to collect the wealth the unbelievers have gathered will not be made available to him in your case because you are marked with the stripes of Christ Jesus. When the power of darkness shall come around and see that you are covered all around by the power of the Lord, they will pass over you and go to someone else (Exodus 12:7–13; Job 1:8–10). However, you must walk in righteousness and holiness, putting the fear of the Lord into everything you do, so that you will prosper and experience divine success and achievements.

Revelation 3:20 says: "Behold, I stand at the door, and knock: if any man hear my voice, and open the door, I will come in to him, and will sup with him, and he with me." Divine success and achievements require obedience to the voice of the Lord, allowing him into your life totally, and finally placing all your plans and endeavors into the hands of the Lord. In return, you will receive spiritual gifts (gold) tried by the fire (imperishable).

## $\mathcal{S}$piritual Meat and Bones Not for Babes

The spiritual meat and bones are meant for those who are truly committed to faith in the Lord and are spiritually awakened. The means for breaking down complex food materials and utilizing their nutrients for growth and activity is weak in (spiritual) babes; hence, they are fed with spiritual milk. Another major concern about eating meat and bones when asleep is the fact that the person will choke, because the major area of the brain for swallowing reflexes is impaired. This is why mothers will not allow their children to eat while sleeping.

I remember one night when dinner was not ready until late in the night. I was very sleepy, but I refused to listen to the cook who advised me to leave the food and go to bed. Instead, I sat down on the floor to eat with both eyes closed and mistakenly rubbed my food against the floor. I learned a big lesson that night because the sleep disappeared at once when I found myself chewing sand and hair.

Those who are spiritually asleep, first and foremost, don't have true access and means to spiritual meat and bones, but they may be given milk. Spiritual meat and bones are the food of those who have gained the power of discernment and understanding for the true power of God. The Apostle Paul wrote: "For every one that useth milk is unskilful in the word of righteousness: for he is a babe. But strong meat belongeth to them that are of full age, even those who by reason of use have their senses exercised to discern both good and evil" (Hebrews 5:13–14).

I want you to pay close attention to the phrase *senses exercised to discern*. What does this phrase mean to you? It is telling you that for you to be able to discern, you must exercise, train, and align your senses to be able to use them for the work of

God. In other words, spiritual discernment requires continual commitment from you daily. When you train yourself on how to utilize the word of God, you obtain divine mastery (knowledge and understanding) through the power of the Holy Spirit working in your life. Continuity and commitment earn you the maturity required to become spiritually sensitized to the Holy Spirit as you work your way into spiritual consciousness.

Physical and spiritual growth both need nutrition and replenishment. Growth is a process, as we are all aware that it requires time as well as other factors. For growth to occur, the conditions for it to take place must be fully satisfied; otherwise, the opposite will take place, which is no growth. The food of the spiritual man is the Word of God. For this reason, those who have little to no comprehension, and those who don't spend time meditating in the Word of God, are spiritual babes and will need to be fed. Remember that babies and those who have their consciousness impaired can't feed themselves. They both need liquid nourishment and will not be able to swallow solid food. The truth is that unbelievers don't spend time reading the Holy Bible; nor will spiritual babes, because they lack motivation to do so and the power to break down the Word to the point of true comprehension.

The Word of God needs more than just comprehension; it must be applied. Application is the task of using information you heard or read in a living context to produce an outcome. The ability to apply scripture repeatedly comes from your true comprehension of what has been presented to your senses. The more you train your senses in the things of truth, righteousness, and holiness, the more spiritually mature (acclimatization) and sensitive they become to the power of God (Holy Spirit).

When the senses are turned-on and plugged into the socket

of the power of God, one no longer needs to be fed again the basic principles of the faith. As you grow spiritually in the faith, the power of God breaks and remakes you to become an outlet for others to connect. When you train yourself to master the principles of the Word of God, you become solid and deeply-rooted in the knowledge of truth. The people of the world are not so; they are spiritually disconnected. Spiritual wakefulness is maintained by your desire to grow in the knowledge of the Word of God and through conformity to principles, laws, and rules of faith. When you seek and train yourself, you will only with time obtain mastery, and according to the apostle Paul, you will attain "full age." With full age comes the ability and understanding to demonstrate the power of God which you have obtained through digestion of the Word of God. The word that you have consumed pushes all you are toward manifestations of God's desire—which is that you grow and become productive.

## The Power of the Word

Spiritual consciousness comes from Jesus Christ, who bestows upon his servants the power of the light. In the physical world, when the sun or a high beam of light is reflected into your eyes, the brain records it as daytime, and your potential to sleep is reduced. Although there are people who will continue to sleep with light directed at them, in such case, unless in sleep deprivation, such individuals need to be medically evaluated for sleep disorder. When sleep disorder is not the issue and all criteria are satisfied, sleeping under a bright light may not occur.

In the Word of God, the light is Jesus Christ, and he is the way. If you have Jesus Christ and his Spirit dwelling in your life, then you have the light of God in you. When you have the light, then your ability to fall asleep is diminished or doesn't exist. Sleep will only come when you consciously decide to yield to it. The power for spiritual sleep is imposed on any person by Satan through seductions and luring. When you yield to the power of spiritual sleep, you are conforming to the power of Satan. For sleep to occur, the light must be removed. When darkness is the ruling power, the senses are disconnected from the socket of God's power and connected to that of Satan. There is a transition point between this transferring and transformation. At this stage the person will still try to resist doing some things that are ungodly, until the resistance (the light power) is expended and there is total darkness. The transition point does vary and may take a short time for some and longer for others. Therefore, a person whose consciousness has been impaired or totally disconnected will find it easy to do things contrary to the will and Word of God.

Light is a form of energy. Light is composed of electromagnetic waves of particles (photons) that travel through space with time. The light of God according to the Holy Scriptures, is greater and brighter than any light put together (Revelation 22:16). This is true as testified to by the Apostle Paul, just before his conviction, on his way to Damascus to capture those who professed Jesus Christ as the Messiah (Acts 9:3–4). He was met on the way by the Lord, and the light that shone upon him was brighter than the daylight. Jesus is the light of God to the world, and he is the word of God. The Word of God is a Light for the righteous, and within it is the power of conviction, which helps align you to live in holiness and truth. The word of God is given unto us for counsel and edification, to nurture, encourage, and enlighten us.

The word *enlighten* can be separated into two parts: *en* and *lighten*. *En* is a prefix meaning "within" or "in" (Dictinary.com);

*lighten,* on the other hand, means "bring to light" or "bring to conscious level." Therefore, if the Word of God enlightens you, it means that it creates within you the power needed for consciousness. When you are conscious, you are in a wakeful and alert state of mind, because of the power of the light of God's Word is working inside of you. Just as a little spark of fire can become a huge flame of fire, so also is the Word of God transformed from a little spark to a great light.

The power of light and of fire is so strong that fire can literally destroy anything along its path. So is the Word of God. The Word of God is a consuming fire, and the natural principles and laws of nature it does not obey, because it is spiritual. The power of the fire of God fell on the altar prepared by the Prophet Elijah, demonstrating God's power as supreme on Mount Camel (1 Kings 18:38). After the prayer was offered by Elijah, the fire of God fell on the altar, which had been soaked with water, as recorded in the Bible. The fire of God fell and consumed all that was put forth and licked up both the water and the dust underneath the altar.

When you have the power of God working in your life, it transforms you into a flaming fire, because you have his word in you. "He makes his angels spirits and his ministers flames of fire" (Hebrews 1:7 NIV.)." We that obey God's words and follow after righteousness and holiness are transformed through the power of the Holy Spirit. The Holy Spirit infuses your life with fire; for this reason, we are encouraged to always pray in the Spirit.

When you pray in the Spirit, you are exercising the power of the Spirit of God. The benefit of continuous exercising, through praying in the Spirit, is the fine-tuning of your senses. When you become sensitized to the power of God, you become more spiritually awake. When spiritually awake, you soon start to exercise the power of discernment; and you will also experience the manifestation of the gift that is assigned to you by God. The gift assigned to you by God is aligned to your purpose and destiny.

The power of the light of God makes you a danger to the power of darkness and Satan. For this reason, Jesus Christ said in Matthew 28:18 and Luke 10:19 that *all the power and authority that he was operating with on Earth to subdue the power of darkness and Satan today has been transferred unto us.* The power for operating in the light of God's power mostly comes from our believing in Jesus Christ; in the contrary, if you don't believe in him than the power of the light will not work in your life as you don't possess it.

As a believer, you need both the light of God (Jesus Christ) and the power for operating in the light of God (Holy Spirit). In several instances in the Holy Bible, the significance of the light of God's Word is demonstrated. The light of God's Word also gives you courage, boldness, and increased faith in Jesus Christ. When you don't believe in Jesus Christ, then you don't have faith. Those who don't have faith can't please God (Hebrews 11:6). You can't please God, your creator, and his Son (Jesus Christ) who has called us all out of the darkness of unbelief. For this same issue of unbelief, and mistrust, the children of Israel in the wilderness all perished because of their unbelief (Numbers 14:29; Hebrews 3:15–19), as God swore that they would not enter the Promised Land (place of rest).

In matters of accountability, adults are held to a higher standard to be more responsible than children in both their judgment and character. Children are not held accountable until eight years of age, which is the beginning of accountability. This is true as they are still children and cannot fully grasp the gravity and consequences of their actions.

Spiritual babes, on the other hand, are held accountable whether they know or not. This is the reason why God gave the Holy Scriptures (Bible), the **B**asic **I**nstruction for the **B**eliever's **L**ife on **E**arth. God gave us the scriptural manual to read and understand. It is true that the spiritual babe, just like the natural baby, does not possess the ability to comprehend and understand both the spoken and written Word of God completely. The power for understanding God's written words is given to you by the Holy Spirit.

You must as a child of God seek to be filled with the Holy Spirit, as this is your duty. The Holy Spirit is a powerful spirit, and his potency when used can be overwhelming, especially for spiritual babies. When you meditate on the Word of God, you will find the hidden power of the knowledge of God. When you meditate on the word of God, you become enlightened and become less prone to fall out of the light of truth. The Word of God gears you to become strong in the faith and in your walk with God. The Word of God protects you from the seductions of Satan and the power of darkness, as you become more sensitive to the Holy Spirit.

## $\mathcal{S}$piritual Babes Can't Retain Spiritual Oil

Oil is a symbol of strength, productivity, protection, and power. It is the Holy Spirit that is working in the oil. In the Christian community, oil markings symbolize the impacting of the seal of God's power into whatever it is applied on. In James 5:14, the Apostle James wrote that whenever somebody is sick, the oil should be applied upon that person. The power of God is what is retained in that oil; as a result, whenever or wherever it is applied, the power of God in the oil is transferred into the body of that person or object.

This act of applying oil is called anointing. The anointing oil has been used since the time of Moses and Aaron. In Exodus chapter 30, God instructed Moses to anoint Aaron and his sons. God also told Moses to anoint specific items for purification and consecration. In Deuteronomy 34:9, Joshua, the son of Nun, was anointed by Moses by the laying on of hands, and it was noted that he became filled with the spirit of wisdom. Hence, you must understand that the impartation of God's power can be accomplished via smearing of anointing-oil, or through laying on of holy hands.

Your ability to hold or retain the power of God is sometimes referred to as an anointing. Being anointed means you are able to retain God's power and utilize it for the works and for the body of Christ (church). For you to retain that anointing power of God, your totality must be submitted and subjected to the power of God. The process of subjecting and submission does take time and commitment; however, the outcome of your obedience is the transformation of your totality into a holy vessel. Only a holy vessel can retain the power of God, as the power of God seals up the porosity that sin creates. In the life of spiritual babes, they cannot retain spiritual oil because their vessels are not fully developed to retain it. This is the reason why the Lord loves the spiritual babes because their vessels can be broken and remolded into the shape that God wants them to be. Those vessels that are unbreakable God will not use, and they cannot be remolded. Just as you will not want to pour your cooking oil into a porous vessel that can never be sealed, so also God will not want to waste spiritual oil on an unmendable vessel that is leaking.

When you give a natural baby oil for food, the baby will experience a purge (nausea and/or diarrhea); this is what also happens to the spiritual babe. In order to prevent malabsorption and indigestion, the Holy Spirit slowly inputs spiritual power into baby Christians so as not to overwhelm them. As you continue in the ways of truth and holiness, God breaks you and remolds your totality. As you continue to walk in the way of the light of God's power, your ability to retain spiritual anointing (power) increases. Your ability to retain more anointing is equivalent to spiritual growth. In other words, growth and maturity in the spiritual is correlated with the ability to retain and demonstrate spiritual power. Those who have failed to grow spiritually will remain as babes, and their ability to retain spiritual power is little. These are people who just keep falling back into sin, while ignorantly removing the seal of God.

The benefit of spiritual anointing is that it increases in you the power of God. Another benefit is that it earns you a place in God's circle of trust. Your ability to hold spiritual power makes you a friend of God and a trustworthy steward. For the same reason Jesus Christ told his disciples that they were no longer servants but friends (John 15:15).

Your ability to hold spiritual anointing makes you a valuable commodity to God and to the body of Christ. According to the Apostle Paul, "In a great house there are not only vessels of gold and of silver, but also of wood and of earth; and some to honour, and some to dishonour. If a man therefore purge himself from these, he shall be a vessel unto honor, sanctified, and meet for the master's use, and prepared unto every good work" (2 Timothy 2:20–21). The key word for you here is *keeping your vessel clean and available*. Holiness and righteousness can only be achieved by keeping yourself clean. When you keep yourself from evil and acts of ungodliness, you become holy; in addition, upon achieving holiness and trust, you still need the Holy Spirit to occupy your vessel. It is the dwelling of the Spirit of God in your vessel that gives you the power and anointing to do the will of God. It is the power of the Holy Spirit retained in your vessel that gives you the ability to do the impossible.

The ministry of Jesus Christ on Earth really began after he was baptized and filled with the Holy Spirit. After he was baptized by John the Baptist; the Holy Spirit descended upon him like a dove (Matthew 3:16; Mark 1:10; Luke 3:22; John 1:32). Upon receiving the Holy Spirit, Jesus Christ began to do the impossible (signs and wonders and miracles). The power for doing the impossible is spiritual, and it comes from the impartation of the Holy Spirit into a person. This fact is true and is demonstrated in the Holy Scriptures in everyone who was filled with the Holy Spirit. King David, after being anointed by the Prophet Samuel, was filled with the Holy Spirit and soon defeated the giant (Goliath of Gath) in a one-on-one battle (1 Samuel 17:50). The Apostle Peter healed the lame man at the Beautiful Gate after receiving the impartation of the Holy Spirit (Acts 3:1–10).

## Spiritual Babes Need the Holy Spirit

Upon receiving Jesus Christ into your life, you are automatically transformed spiritually, and you obtain salvation. For complete transformation and regeneration to occur, Jesus Christ told Nicodemus:

> Verily, verily, I say unto thee, Except a man be born again, he cannot see the kingdom of God.

> Nicodemus saith unto him, How can a man
> be born when he is old? can he enter the second
> time into his mother's womb, and be born?
>
> Jesus answered, Verily, verily, I say unto thee,
> Except a man be born of water and of the Spirit,
> he cannot enter into the kingdom of God. That
> which is born of the flesh is flesh; and that which
> is born of the Spirit is spirit. (John 3:3–6)

Being born-again refers to the regeneration or rebirth of your spiritual man. Regeneration begins inside of you and can only take place when you accept the Lord into your life. Due to the fact that regeneration starts from the inside and works its way out, many people may feel that nothing has changed in their lives. What they don't realize is that they have been spiritually awakened.

Regeneration and transformation are both continuous processes, but they start instantaneously when you repent. Just as a seed needs time to grow into a tree, so also is the process of repentance and transformation. Remember, also for a vessel to be broken and remolded to a shape desired by God does take time, patience, and consistency. The progression and advancement period for spiritual development needs your full participation and commitment. Another very important step that should never be overlooked is the vocal confession of sins and repentance (2 Corinthians 7:10), both initially and anytime a fall back into sin occurs. Upon completion of the initial confession and repentance, your spiritual man comes alive, and like a baby just brought forth from the womb, you will need spiritual nourishment.

Spiritual nourishment comes from the Word of God. I will

stress this matter again: *Spiritual nourishment comes from the word of God.* The spiritual baby must strive to grow and to keep his or her vessel clean. You must walk in love just like Jesus Christ. When operating in love, you're demonstrating both the fear of God and a desire to be his child (again, like Jesus Christ). Your growing desire to know him and to seek his face draws you closer to God. Your love for God helps you put into action your fear of him. This is what attracts the power of God to you and gives room for the Holy Spirit to grow inside your heart. With the Holy Spirit working in your life, your spiritual man will learn to resist sin and seek after righteousness. It is the power of the Holy Spirit that is working in you that will allow you to demonstrate true fear and obtain spiritual understanding from God (Proverbs 7:1–3). Without understanding the spiritual babe can't fully grasp the importance of living a holy life and the consequences of specific deeds. The lack of understanding is what allows a lot of believers to continue in the pathway of rebellion and disobedience.

## Power for Spiritual Wakefulness

The power for spiritual awakening spurs Christ consciousness in you. The power for spiritual wakefulness to resist Satan, the devil, comes from the Holy Spirit (Acts 11:16). In John 14-16 Jesus told his disciples that he would send us a comforter who would teach us and let us know God's mind (see Acts 2). This is the only way you can tell your spiritual state in the first place. Second, Jesus Christ did instruct the Apostles that they should go and preach the gospel (evangelize) and baptizing the people (in water and the power of the Holy Spirit). This mandate he gave to us, and it requires that every believer should receive both the water baptism (baptism by immersion) and the baptism of fire (the Holy Spirit)—no exceptions. If you are a believer and follower of Jesus Christ, you must not only be baptized in water, but you must also receive the gift of speaking in tongues, which is the power of God's Spirit (baptism of the Holy Spirit).

## Walk in the Light of God's Power

Your walk with God earns you spiritual power and authority over every other power. The power and authority which you as a believer of Jesus Christ now possess in your vessel can only be given to you by him. I will stress this matter again and again, because many believers soon forget their spiritual identity and by whose power they are operating against the power of darkness. Jesus Christ said to the apostles and to us as well: "the power and authority which was given to me by my Father in heaven; this I give unto you" (see Luke 10:19). He also said that we are to use it to step on every serpent and scorpions, and every power of darkness—including Satan.

The power Jesus Christ is referring to is the power of the Holy Spirit. It is the power of the Holy Spirit that takes you into spiritual heights. Upon attaining spiritual heights through the power of the Holy Spirit you received, you will discover that each time you visit a certain area, people will quickly take their bags and run away or will not be able to do what they used to do before you came. Another sign that you have the power of God working in your life is experiencing people going out of their way to favor you. The Bible clearly states, "The Lord makes his angels spirits and his ministers flames of fire" (see Psalm 104:4; Hebrews 1:7). Wonder no more when or why people stare at you. When you connect yourself to God's power, things begin to transform in your favor and to the glory of the Lord.

The Holy Spirit on several occasions has shown me that there are people using demonic powers to work their way to the top level of their careers at the expense of innocent souls who are standing by, not knowing what is going on around them. This is the reason every child of the living God needs to step out of spiritual slumber and arise. You need to arise through prayers: to conquer and take possession of what the cross and the blood of Jesus Christ have obtained for you. The blood of Jesus Christ gives us a permanent anchorage to the covenant and promises of God.

Galatians 5:25 states: "If we live in the Spirit, let us also walk in the Spirit." If you believe and claim to have the most powerful spirit (the Holy Spirit) dwelling in you as a child of God Most High, you are therefore instructed to walk in the Spirit. The Word of God is Spirit, and it is life; it quickens and edifies the spiritual man and the body. The Word of God is Jesus Christ, who is the light of the world. If you have his light working in your life, you will not walk in darkness; nor will Satan and the power of sin and disobedience be able to lure you into engaging in ungodly impulses to satisfy a lust. To yield to that lust is to compromise your faith.

Compromising your faith brings forth fruits of rebellion and sin. Whenever you sin, you sin not only against yourself (body, soul, and spirit) but also against the cross (Jesus Christ, and the Holy Spirit). Most of all, you sin against God, your Father in heaven. I pray upon your life today that the Holy Spirit will give you power to walk in the light of Jesus Christ. I also pray that the Holy Spirit will bestow upon your life the power to live a holy life and that you will not obey Satan. I pray that the power of God increases and awakens your senses to know him and love him genuinely. I pray your consciousness and conscience be awakened that you will heed and obey the voice of God. In Jesus Christ's name I pray, amen.

# *T*he Rod for Correction

Whenever you sin, you are not only staining your spiritual armor; you are crucifying Jesus Christ a second time (Hebrews 6:4–6) as well as casting down your identity as a child of God. Casting down your spiritual authority and power—all of this results from disobedience. If you pray for forgiveness, you are immediately forgiven, but a punishment is still given; consequences still follow.

Sometimes we are unaware of just when God is chastising us. That is why many believers lose many things without being aware that a miracle or an opportunity has just passed by them. God is a just God. He is not partial, and the purpose for correction is that we may learn and grow to understand his will and operations. Correction makes you stronger and solidifies your love in the knowledge of God's power to hate and stay away from sin. Correction helps you remain in the pathway of holiness and cease from always praying the prayers of repentance. God corrects you so that you learn to resist Satan, and when you resist Satan, he will flee from you.

You must resist the devil through prayers and faith (the Word of God). If you are still falling short, then you must take it to the next level of spiritual warfare, which is prayer and fasting. Jesus Christ made this clear to the apostles who were trying to cast out a demon from a child who was possessed, stating that this type of spirit would not go except with prayer and fasting (see Matthew 17:21; Mark 9:29).

If you are still being tormented or tempted by Satan, I want you never to lose hope, because you are not alone. I encourage you to take such matters to your spiritual father in the Lord, or find a believing church where you can find help. This I say because when two or more prayer warriors are assisting you in prayers, the battles become easy and results are obtained more quickly (Matthew 18:20).

## Discernment through the Holy Spirit

Alertness and wakefulness come from the Holy Spirit of God. The ability for knowing is called discernment. Discernment is a spiritual gift. The ability to discern occurs when there is a relay of messages between the supernatural and the natural senses. The spiritual senses (heart, eyes, mouth, ears, and hand) are controlled by the power of the Holy Spirit. Clearly stated, anybody who has the power of discernment is operating in a state of spiritual consciousness and wakefulness. This spiritual power is imparted into you when you receive the Holy Spirit. The purpose for this is to allow you to see, observe, hear, feel, and know what specific action God requires you to take if it is needed, and when to do so.

These days people are so caught up in watching TV and listening to loud music that it is difficult for most people to hear from God and the Holy Spirit. Some of these new technologies are intended to make people less sensitive to the things of God and the Holy Spirit. These gadgets are made to occupy and suspend your senses (eyes, ears, mind, and heart). I encourage you to spend time in God's presence, as this only takes a small portion of your time. The more time you spend in the presence of God, the faster you climb the ladder of divine power transformation—becoming more like him.

Discernment is a gift from God, operated through the Holy Spirit. Remember that it is also the power of the Holy Spirit that helps you connect and utilize spiritual talents. The spiritual talents bestowed upon you when you were created in the womb depend mostly on your spiritual purpose and functioning in the house of God. The more frequently you are doing God's work, and the closer your divine assignment is to the altar, the more abundantly the power of discernment is apportioned to you. Some are given this gift with little to no association with the altar, but they may have a divine assignment that they need to do. This is a true saying, because in the house of God there are many vessels, and each one has a function and purpose. Just as in the kitchen, there are vessels that have similar functions, and many have purposes and functions that diverge from the others.

"Brethren, we are debtors, not to the flesh, to live after the flesh" (Romans 8:12). As true worshippers and believers of Jesus Christ, we are indebted to the services and doing the work of God. We must demonstrate devotedness in our actions and attitude as believers. We must surrender our hearts completely to the services and works of the church, which is the body of Christ. By surrendering our totality, we make ourselves available to be used by God as instruments and vessels consecrated for the works of the house of Lord, which is the church.

In addition, as consecrated vessels, we should without murmuring or delays, endeavor to complete our divine assignment on earth in all diligence and fear of God. It is required of every believer to daily spend time, no matter how short, in

God's presence in prayer and worship. What matters to the Holy Spirit is our compliance and love for God's instruction—which is our faith and shield. Worshipping God is a powerful spiritual instrument often known to us as "praise." Praising God through worship songs and psalms brings to you the glory of God. I encourage you to do this as often as possible. Where there is no room for Satan to dwell, there is no room for him to work in your life.

The Bible clearly states that God's purposes are achieved not by works alone but by faith. As stated earlier, faith comes by believing and trusting in the Lord. Faith is putting your hope and trust in things neither seen nor perceived. Faith is hoping and trusting in the unknown, which is the power of God. Your faith comes from seeds that were sown into your life through the Word of God you received (heard and read). It is the power in the Word of God working inside you that transforms you to become a tree of righteousness. As a plant in God's vineyard, you are to produce fruits with seeds of righteousness. The seed of righteousness is the word of God you impart into other people's lives through your actions and attitude. Wrong actions and attitude are the reason why many trees never bear fruit.

In the Parable of the Sower (Matthew 13:1–23; Mark 4:1–20; Luke 8:4–15), the seeds fell on different types of soil. The soil plays a major part in the outcome of that seed (becoming a sprout), and also it determines what will happen to the sprout (continuity of that plant becoming a tree). The period when the seed is transforming into a tree is filled with challenges; so also is this period in a believer's life. Satan will try to kill the plant, so it will not grow; and if it does grow, he will try to stop it from bearing fruit. Remember, when a tree is corrupted either it will not bear fruit, or it will produce fruits of unrighteousness. Those who maintain their faith and belief in Jesus Christ, following after what is good, will bear fruit (seeds of righteousness) pleasing in the sight of the Lord. The fruits depict your fervency and persistence in the faith and works. Remember that it is not only by acts of righteousness you are granted eternal life in Jesus Christ but above all by your faith in him.

Temptations, trials, and tribulations on Earth are things that all Christians should expect in their walk with God. When you are being tempted or tried, know that you are not alone. Satan is doing everything possible to keep many away from the pathway of faith and from trusting God. That is why the Bible says: "Resist the devil, and he will flee from you" (James 4:7).

To resist the devil, you need to exercise "faith power." To exercise faith power, first, you need to repent of your sins; second, you need to get filled with the Holy Spirit; third, you need to spend time meditating on God's Word; fourth, you need to spend time engaging yourself in fasting and praying. Upon doing all these things, you have to abstain or keep yourself from every appearance (seed of unrighteousness) that is not edifying to your spiritual man. The spiritual man in you is awakened when you give your life to Jesus Christ. To keep the spiritual man inside you alive, you need faith power from the Word of God and the Holy Spirit.

As a believing Christian, you must continue to train and make yourself more acquainted with the Word of God and his operations. You are also expected to develop sensitivity to the power of Holy Spirit. With your commitment and persistence, there will come a point where the sinful nature that was operating in you is diminished. The resistance you used to feel toward God's word and power are also diminished; however, you must continue in the pathway of righteousness and holiness.

Your walk with the Lord on this earth is not complete until you take your last breath or until his return. If either of these events has not occurred, you are to remain steadfast in the pathway of faith. You are to do everything that pleases God and strengthen your relationship with him. You must demonstrate a strong desire to know him more and seek to know his mind through personal training of your spiritual senses. As your spiritual senses attain maturity (mastery), the voice of the Holy Spirit becomes clear and loud; following God's instructions will no longer be a burden; and being in the presence of God becomes an enjoyable task.

Another benefit of spiritual maturity is an increase in the knowledge of God's Word. You will start to understand that the Word of the Lord is your sword and shield. If faith comes by hearing and meditating on the Word of God, this clearly means that the Word of God is meant to equip you. If the Word of God is a sword (Hebrews 4:12), then faith is a weapon that each believer carries spiritually. Faith is a weapon to defend and to fight and can never be your currency. Our spiritual currency is righteousness. Our hope and faith is built on Jesus Christ, for the Bible says that without faith we cannot please God (Hebrews 11:6). Secondly, you can't buy God's favor, but rather you obtain it, as it is given freely to those who exercise their trust (faith) in the Lord.

## Your Duty as a Child of God

Faith is enhanced by the words you hear. Faith is also empowered and effective when you hear the testimonies of other believers. It is the power of God manifesting in the lives of believers and people who have experienced a positive outcome through exercising faith. Faith is exercised or expressed by your attitude; hence the fact that faith is a muscle and not currency. Our Lord and Savior, Jesus Christ, during his ministry on Earth, often mentioned to his disciples and to others around him that if anybody has faith as small as a mustard seed (which is one of the smallest seeds), they have the power that can move mountains. These mountains are moved by your belief in the Word of God, as well as exercising the power in the Word of God. Through your belief in God, you are able to carry out the impossible. Doing the impossible, obviously, is the demonstrating and exercising God's power. In addition, the Bible clearly states that without faith we cannot please God. Jesus Christ often said: "What I see my Father in heaven doing that is what I do; what I hear my Father in heaven saying, that is what I speak to you (John 5:19)." When you are acting in faith you are expressing that divine character that was bestowed freely upon your spiritual man by the Holy Ghost. This characters also includes courage and bold aligned in the knowledge of God's power through Jesus Christ.

The Word of God is power, it is fire, and it is life. In the Book of Genesis, God is revealed as the God who calls into existence those things that are not in existence. Remember, we are the children of God, made in his image and likeness. Therefore, as a true child of God who possesses his power (the Holy Spirit), you are expected to exercise the power in you by demonstrating faith. If faith is the Word of God you hear, therefore, as a tree of righteousness planted in God's vineyard, your roots and source of spiritual nourishment depends solely on your anchorage in the word of God.

In God's vineyard you are a tree planted by the rivers of living water (Psalm 1:3; Jeremiah 17:8). The living water is the word of God, which is Jesus Christ. Jesus said: "I am the living water: let those who thirst come and drink of this water that I alone can give, and they will never thirst again" (John 4:13–14 paraphrased). Those who shall drink of this water will never thirst again because the water of life is the power of God, which is also the Word of God. As a tree planted by that living water, you become filled with God's power, and all you need to do is to bear fruit.

The natural tree brings fruits in due season, and it depends on the natural forces of nature and the environment (soil nutrients and water in the soil) to produce. In respect to a believer there is no due season. The fruit you bring forth as a believing Christian is the product of your faith and the supernatural power of God working in you. As a tree planted in God's house, you are expected to bring forth fruit regardless of season. According to Word of God, any tree that does not bring forth fruit shall be cut down and cast into fire.

Every time we are demonstrating faith in our behaviors and attitude, we are acting just like our Father in heaven. Hence the word: "like father; like son." If we are children of God, made in his image and likeness, we are expected to act and operate just like him. This statement is true because we have his genes and his spirit dwelling inside us. The faith you express at a time leads to a positive outcome, and the products are the fruit you bear. The fruit is a result of the genes' source, and the seed is a part of the fruit and not the whole. The fruit contains seed(s) that contain within them the power for the next generation.

For the continuity of the gospel, as well as being a believer, we are all expected to disperse seeds of faith into people's lives. There are many seeds, and imprinted in the seeds you bear is the power of God. Sowing seeds into the lives of other people and into the church **by your actions** creates an atmosphere of righteousness which is profitable for the movement of God's power. In such an environment you will experience testimonies in your life, as well as in the lives of people around you. In an environment filled with trees of righteousness, you will observe true spiritual growth in your walk with God, because his power is filling you and nourishing you. In such an environment, where the power and Spirit of God dwells, the people are led and walk in the Spirit. Those who are led by the Spirit of God are the children of God (Romans 8:14). In such an environment, God's power takes over your totality, and you will no longer be afraid of what people will say or do to you. As a result of his power and Spirit operating in you, you will come out in boldness and confidence. It is that springing out in boldness and true love for God that pushes you to witness to others about Jesus Christ, the hope of glory. The power and Spirit of God growing in your life allow you to develop an unshakable love and compassion for all humanity. The compassion and love of God for humanity dwelling in your life is what will propel you to speak to others about the coming back of the Messiah; about repentance; about forgiveness, mercy, and grace; and about the judgment of God to come. If you claim to be your brother's and sister's keeper, you must tell them the truth no matter the situation. You must speak the truth to them even if they don't want to hear about Jesus Christ.

## They Are Led by the Spirit of God

In Luke 2:22–40, you will read about two people who were led and filled with the Holy Spirit. They were the righteous and devout Simeon and the Prophetess Anna. According to what is written of them, they were filled with the Holy Spirit. As surprising as it may sound is the fact that at time, Jesus Christ was still a baby. You will read that they were both led by the Holy Spirit into the temple because they were grounded in the power of God. As verse 37 points out, the Prophetess Anna spent time separating herself for the impartation of the power of God into her life. We read that she spent her days in thorough prayers and fasting. These people saw the light of God and were filled with the Holy Spirit.

The natural light is very important for natural trees to grow and bring forth fruits. In the spiritual life of a believer, Jesus Christ is the light of God. So we might remain in the light, Jesus Christ gave us a companion, the Holy Spirit. For you to operate in the light of God's power, you must receive or be imparted with the gift of speaking in tongues. If you have not received it yet, I encourage you to do so as soon as possible.

In the Book of Acts, chapter 2, you will read that after the disciples and those around them in the upper-room, on the day of Pentecost, had received the Holy Spirit, the apostle Peter spoke out boldly. Remember, the Apostles (Jesus's inner circle) were hiding themselves from the public. Upon being endued with the power of the Holy Spirit, the apostles kicked fear aside and came out of hiding to speak and teach about Jesus Christ in confidence and boldness. This is the true nature of the power of the light of God, which is intended to transform you.

When God transforms you, everything about you is broken and remolded. You should never be afraid of anything, because God has not given unto us the spirit of fear. Rather, God has given us the spirit of courage, love, boldness, power, and a sound mind (see 2 Timothy 1:7). All these are a result of God's impartation which is working in you when you receive the Holy Spirit. In addition, your totality becomes grounded in the power of God's

Word and will. Hence the need for spending time in praying, fasting, and meditating on the Word of God.

One day I was almost running late for a Sunday service. It had snowed throughout the night, and I knew that my car would be covered. For one reason or another, my gloves were missing and not in their usual place. After searching for almost ten minutes; I opened my mouth and asked the Holy Spirit to help me locate them. Immediately I had finished that prayer, I heard the Holy Spirit say to me, "Go to your study table." I obeyed the voice and stood by the table. He moved my hands to push one of the books on the table aside, and there were the gloves staring back at me. If I had not asked for help, I would never have imagined leaving the gloves between books on the table and not where they belonged.

## $\mathcal{T}$he Power for Consistency

Some people, even believers, have the false belief that they will not be held accountable for their actions, even if they do not know certain things. I have heard some people teaching and saying these words as well. Such teaching diminishes and prevents (diverts) people from seeking the truth. The truth is that we are held accountable whether we have our eyes and ears closed or not.

Your daily duty is to devote time to gather information from your Bible. The Bible is the **B**asic **I**nstruction for the **B**eliever's **L**ife on **E**arth. Before you went to a driving school, you had to study what you need to know about driving. You read about the road signs, rules, and regulations of driving. So also, whatever your occupation may be, you got some form of information and orientation before you started the job. The Bible is your basic instruction on Earth, and you are required to spend time to seek out what God wants you to know. God speaks to us daily, but we get carried away and entangle ourselves with so much activity that we totally forget about who we are—our spiritual identity. We are consumed with being busy until something goes wrong; then we remember that God still exists. This pattern of forgetting about God and remembering when trouble arises is what you will read and see repeatedly in the Bible.

> And Joshua the son of Nun, the servant of the Lord, died, being an hundred and ten years old. And they buried him in the border of his inheritance in Timnathheres, in the mount of Ephraim, on the north side of the hill Gaash. And also all that generation were gathered unto their fathers: and there arose another generation after them, which knew not the Lord, nor yet the works which he had done for Israel.
>
> And the children of Israel did evil in the sight of the Lord, and served Baalim: and they forsook the Lord God of their fathers, which brought them out of the land of Egypt, and followed other gods, of the gods of the people that were round about them, and bowed themselves unto them, and provoked the Lord to anger. And they forsook the Lord, and served Baal and Ashtaroth. And the anger of the LORD was hot against Israel, and he delivered them into the hands of spoilers that spoiled them, and he sold them into the hands of their enemies round about, so that they could not any longer stand before their enemies. Whithersoever they went out, the hand of the

Lord was against them for evil, as the Lord had
said, and as the Lord had sworn unto them: and
they were greatly distressed. (Judges 2:8–15)

In this passage we read that, after Joshua and those who saw the
power of God in the wilderness had all died, the people forgot
about God and made to themselves idols—repeating what they
had done in the wilderness at the time of Moses and Aaron. They
went from a state of spiritual wakefulness to spiritual slumber
and disobedience. We're told in verses 14–15 that God took away
the covering of protection from them and allowed their enemies
to oppress them. God himself fought against them, because they
turned and worshipped idols of the people driven out of the land
for the same reason.

I pray in Jesus's name that this will never be our portion.
When God is against a person or nation, nothing can save such
a soul or country. Today, many people are working much as the
Israelites did after the death of Joshua. The hunger for God and
love for the truth (holiness and righteousness) is diminishing
daily as people are doing whatever pleases their heart. As the
Apostle Paul wrote about the last days, people will be seekers
of pleasure and have little regard for the word of God and
instruction (see 2 Timothy 3:2–5).

Those who are filled with God's power are led by his Spirit,
just like the Prophet Simeon and the Prophetess Anna, as we
read in the Book of Luke. Being led means that the power of God,
which is the power of Christ consciousness, is working in you.
I encourage you to please pick up your Bible and find out what
you need to be doing before the judgment of God comes, when
there will be no excuses.

**As ye know how we exhorted and comforted and charged every one of you, as a father doth his children, that ye would walk worthy of God, who hath called you unto his kingdom and glory. (1 Thessalonians 2:11–12)**

The desire of the Lord (Jesus Christ) is to see men, women, and children walk worthy and acceptable to our Father in Heaven (God), who gave his only beloved son to die for us. The desire of the Lord is to see us grow to know our heavenly Father (God) and be saved. For this reason, he gave us his Word (the Old Testament—the law, wisdom books, and prophets—and the New Testament).

God's expectation is that all who search and long for him should find him. For this purpose, Jesus Christ said, "I am the light of the world. Whoever follows me will never walk in darkness" (John 8:12 NIV). You will not walk in darkness because he (Jesus Christ) shall be your light and his Word a staff to guide you to the truth. In Jesus Christ is the true nature and attribute of God's power revealed: love, truth, righteousness, holiness, faithfulness, mercy, grace, hope, and life. All these God wants to share with you and with all who are lost to sin, as an expiation so that all may return to the former nature. Second, God's intention is that all be saved from his wrath and judgment to come upon this world and upon those who did not believe in Jesus Christ.

# ❧ 7 ❧

# The Rules, Laws, and Principles (RLPs) of Faith

In the journey of life, every man or woman takes certain things with them. These are tools used as aids to guide them when making decisions. These tools also reflect your place of birth, experiences, observations, traditions, and customs. In a word, your personal tool consists of your belief system and its operation. All belief systems and their operational effectiveness are based on a person's perception and conceptual robustness. As a believer your conceptual robustness is enhanced and modified because the Holy Spirit gives you that leverage. In the spiritual and physical there are rules, laws, and principles (RLPs); they serve not just as tools but also as a compass to guide you through daily life events. In the world we live in, when your compass is either broken or lost, your RLPs operations lead to disaster.

Within the Word of God are the RLPs that must be learned, and mastery is essential because they need be applied properly in every situation in which we find ourselves. The human RLPs are based on several factors put together to create a way of living and approaching life as an individual. The makeup of an individual's RLPs include tribe, religious practices, occultism, and regional and societal experiences. Most human RLPs are those things that have been passed down to us. These RLPs have been developed for generations. These rules, laws, and principles were retained because they were profitable to the people who used them.

Similarly, God's intention for salvation is intertwined into his rules, laws, and principles (RLPs). In addition, other criteria must be satisfied to the maximum for completeness. Put together, the criteria and the RLPs make up the Word of God. In other words, within the Word of God there is just more to it than his rules, laws, and principles. Therefore, whenever you apply yourself to God's Word, the outcome of such an action is that you become part and parcel of his will. When you are locked into God's will, it gears and propels you toward fulfilling your divine destiny upon this earth.

The Word of God is Spirit, it is light, and it is life (Jesus Christ). It incorporates the power of Holy Spirit. When the Word of God is working within your life, the power within it takes possession of both your natural body and your spiritual man dwelling inside your body. The level of control that God (the Holy Spirit) has on you is based on your yielding and your daily doings. Your daily doings consist of your obedience to prayers, meditations on God's Word, and resisting sin.

Simply put, what makes you obey the laws, rules, and principles is the Holy Spirit. The Holy Spirit is also a teacher and a companion. As a teacher, the Holy Spirit instructs you based on the Word of God you meditate on. The Holy Spirit teaches you how and when to apply the RLPs. As your companion and friend, the Holy Spirit will teach you how to use the Holy Scriptures to communicate with God through prayers. The Word of God is life, and these words you pray come alive. The words come alive because they are the Word of God, and within it is the secret power to defeat Satan, when the secrets are unlocked. When the Word of God comes alive, it bestows upon your life divine wisdom and understanding needed to quench the power of confusion and chaos.

Contrary to the laws, rules, and principles of God are those of Satan and the power of darkness in this world. These are all grounded in the agenda of Satan, which is to make sure that nobody fulfills their divine destiny. Satan is a deceiver whose intention is to make many people go against the promises of God and be kept away from the truth. Satan perverts the truth and seduces people to follow his rules, laws, and principles. The satanic RLPs have been in existence for millennia, and some have somehow found their way into our society, cultural practices, lifestyles, and communities.

The RLPs of Satan are grounded in confusion and chaos. Just as the Holy Spirit is working in those yielded to the Word of God, so also those who restrain themselves from following righteousness are enslaved to the power of darkness and Satan. The power of darkness deludes such people to be comfortable with sin, seeing the Word of God as inconveniencing, burdensome, boring, and a waste of time. These are the people who spend lots of money drinking alcohol, gambling, and feeding drug addictions. These people live a life filled with immoralities and enjoy doing things that are inconvenient and against God's intended purpose for their life.

Who then implements satanic rules, laws, and principles? Satanic RLPs are enforced by demonic spirits on their subjects at specific times. The mission of these spirits is to manipulate a person's life with an intention to prevent, steal, destroy, or kill their destiny. They also try to frustrate, and if they can, they will make that person fail to reach heaven. The majority of this spirit attack is directed against Christians and true believers who are at lower states of consciousness. The agenda behind satanic RLPs is to make you an ineffective follower of Jesus Christ.

The powers enforcing satanic RLPs set you up to engage in things that are sinful. It is these demonic spirits that diminish your conscience and console you with lies, even if you personally fail to acknowledge the truth. A good example is working in an office where one of the workers abuses privileges or steals money from the office to purchase food or gifts for co-workers. If those co-workers know this fact but turn a blind eye, they partake in the outcome of that sinful act. This is just an example of how taking part in such a thing exposes you to attacks from these spirits. They will console you to accept it, as other people are doing it; however, based on God's RLPs, it is totally wrong. Whenever you resist and don't partake in such an act, these spirits cannot attack you.

Another thing that can expose you as a believer to the powers of demonic spirits is your roots and background. Your background draws on your ancestors and their beliefs. Thank God for the blood of Jesus that was shed; whenever you give your life to Jesus Christ, the curses are broken. For you to continue to experience freedom given to you by the blood of Jesus Christ and from demonic spirit attacks, you must remain in the faith without wavering. Remember, Jesus taught that when the demons possessing a person are cast out of that individual, they (the demons) go and dwell in dry places and will try to come back into that person's life (Matthew 12:43-45 & Luke11:24). They can repossess a person or attack only when the individual is still engaging in sin. The Bible calls sin "the little foxes that spoil the vines" (Song of Solomon 2:15). When these demonic spirits regain access into a person, they will reinstate whatever RLPs previously operated in the person's life. The life and circumstances surrounding such a person get rough and can be worse than before they were believers. To prevent this detrimental situation, Jesus Christ warns that we should remain committed to the acts of holiness and righteousness, as this prevents demonic reentry and stops satanic access into your life.

Evil RLPs are enforced by spiritual wickedness and by Satan, and they are against any person who identifies or is called a child of God. As an awake Christian you are not immune to spiritual attacks and temptation. When these demonic spirits don't have direct access to your life, they will attack your spiritual power indirectly.

Their two major tactics are to stop your meditations on the holy Bible and your prayer altar. These demonic powers are behind what makes you weak in your prayer life. They are also doing everything possible to prevent you from meditating on God's Word. These spirits bring bad luck, failures, frustrations, sadness, disappointments, and backsliding. These spirits are the ones who will try to convince you that God has forgotten about you. These are the spirits that will tell you to go into fornication or adultery. These spirits will tell you to lie or steal when no one is watching.

These demonic spirits do many other things as well; they can lure you into harboring malice, expressing anger, and fighting with even your fellow believers or church leaders. These spirits will make you resistant to correction. These spirits will fill your heart and mind with thoughts and attitudes meant to increase suspicion and mistrust and even to make you drive away your spiritual and physical helpers. The demonic spirits do all this if you allow them to capture your heart and gain your attention. Through dialogue, they will engage you into obeying or yielding to their directives.

These demonic spirits were there in the Garden of Eden and seduced Eve to disobey God's instruction. These spirits have been on this Earth, having existed before the creation of mankind, and they understand spiritual RLPs. They are very aware that "***the wages of sin is death***" (see Romans 6:23).

God's desire is to save mankind and to give us life through Jesus Christ. On the contrary, Satan's desire is to do everything for everyone born on this Earth not to be saved from the wrath and judgment of God to come. God through his son, Jesus Christ, gave us the Holy Spirit to help us to break away from the power of sin and rebellion. The power of sin and rebellion rules and dwells in our natural body. Through Jesus Christ's death and resurrection, God has put a restraining effect on all avenues previously used by Satan and the power of darkness to institute RLPs on those who believe in him and are saved.

God's ultimate aim is for all to be saved. God's RLPs are to guide you to the truth. God's RLPs bring you closer to him. The more time you spend around God, the more he will fill you up with his power and Spirit, which is the Holy Spirit. God's RLPs bring peace and create an atmosphere of true love and friendship. They create love, because God himself is full of love, as you will observe in his operations. His love is unshakable and unwavering, and he loves and cares for you and for everybody; that is why he gave his only son (Jesus Christ). God's RLPs create friendship, because all who believe in Jesus Christ and follow his word become friends of God. As friends and children of God, we become joint heirs of his kingdom. As joint heirs of

God's kingdom, we are to operate in the power of God on Earth just as Jesus Christ did.

Those who are filled with the Holy Spirit can do nothing else than to walk in the Spirit. They walk in the Spirit because they have personally taken time out to fellowship and do God's will through separating themselves in fasting, praying, meditation on scripture, and evangelizing. These operations, carried out with a whole heart yielded to God's RLPs, earn them a deeper anchorage. Anchorage is the connection to the source of God's power, which only increases the manifestation of his power in your life. These people, according to the holy Bible, are vessels of the Lord, and they are trees of righteousness. These individuals have working inside of them the true nature and power of God. These people become so filled with the anointing of God's power that it begins to flow through them. They enact God's RLP upon anyone they encounter. These are people who will never have time to engage in ungodly conversations but will only speak with an intention to bring God's light into your life.

When the light of God comes into any place, the outcome is that darkness flees. Where there is light, everything that is hidden comes to light. As the power of God's light penetrates, it drives away the power of darkness. Jesus Christ our Lord said: "You are the light of the world" (see Matthew 5:14). As true believers and followers of Jesus Christ, we are the light of the world and the children of God Most High. As children of light, we are in the world, but not of this world. As children of the light, we must be of good character, examples of true love and kindness. You must always be willing to help and to share the good news with other people, no matter who they are or their origin. We are to watch our conversation, however, guiding them with God's RLPs so we don't fall for the trickiness or traps of Satan. We should always be ready to learn, to teach, and to be teachable. We should be open to criticism from others even when our expectations are otherwise. We are to encourage others and those who are weak. We must be ready to pray with and for those who are in need or sick, relying on the Holy Spirit.

# 8

## The Consequences of Spiritual Sleep in the Last Days.

5 Thus saith the Lord; Cursed be the man that trusteth in man, and maketh flesh his arm, and whose heart departeth from the Lord.

6 For he shall be like the heath in the desert, and shall not see when good cometh; but shall inhabit the parched places in the wilderness, in a salt land and not inhabited.

7 Blessed is the man that trusteth in the Lord, and whose hope the Lord is.

8 For he shall be as a tree planted by the waters, and that spreadeth out her roots by the river, and shall not see when heat cometh, but her leaf shall be green; and shall not be careful in the year of drought, neither shall cease from yielding fruit.

> ⁹ **The heart is deceitful above all things, and**
> **desperately wicked: who can know it?**
> ¹⁰ **I the Lord search the heart, I try the reins,**
> **even to give every man according to his ways,**
> **and according to the fruit of his doings.**
> **(Jeremiah 17:5-10 KJV)**

In the last days, the requirement for anybody to be saved from the coming wrath of God is to trust and obey the Lord. The promises of God are sure, and he will do everything to bring his Word to be revealed as written. God wants us to understand him and his purpose and to experience his love. For you to believe, you must settle in your heart that whatever God is presenting before you is the truth and not lies. Second, trust is made manifest through acknowledgment with total understanding. Third, understanding comes from the heart, and from the heart, which is dwelling place of the Holy Spirit, comes the Word (Voice) of truth (Proverbs 3:5–6). Because he is your Shepherd, your light, and your maker, you are to trust in the Lord with your whole heart and depend not on your understanding. The world is filled with darkness (disobedience), and to see where you are heading, you need the Light (Jesus Christ), the Word of God (his staff to defend you, and it is your sword and shield), and his companionship (the Holy Spirit).

The prophet Jeremiah said unto the people of Judah as instructed by the Lord: "Thus saith the Lord; Cursed be the man that trusteth in man, and maketh flesh his arm, and whose heart departeth from the Lord" (Jeremiah 17: 5). I want you to pay close attention to the words here. The Lord said cursed be anyone (1) *who trusts in man*; (2) *who makes flesh his arm*; and (3) *whose heart departs from the Lord.*

I have heard many people reference the Old Testament as Old School. I encourage you not to listen to such a person. The holy Bible is given to us in its totality to teach and instruct us in our daily walk with the Lord. Do not let anybody prevent you from getting a total understanding (extracted from God's Word) of what is going on around you and of things you need to know.

Comparing the three important phrases in Jeremiah as highlighted above to the three items from the Proverbs quotation (3:5–6), you will acquire a better understanding why the Lord said such a person is cursed.

*(Jeremiah 17:5)* ← Contrast To → *(Proverbs 3:5–6)*

Man trusted in men (creation) ← Contrary To → Man trusted the Lord (Jesus Christ the light)

ake flesh his arm (Staff, sword and Shield) ← Contrary To → *ex*The Word of God (Staff, sword & Shield)

*whose heart departed from the Lord* ← Contrary To → Companionship (the Holy Spirit)

What the Lord by the instruction of the Holy Spirit wants you to see from the highlights above is that we as believers should learn to trust in him (his Word). The contrary, which is based mostly on men's understanding, can be misleading. Jesus Christ our Lord called it the "blind leading the blind" (Matthew 15:14), and the end is disastrous.

The second point is that the Word of God, as stated earlier is for your instruction, a staff and a light that are intended to lead you in the pathway of righteousness, holiness, and faith. The last point is what makes a lot of people fall into a state of spiritual sleep and slumber because it comes upon its victim quietly: sin and turning away of the heart. A believer who enjoys the company of unbelievers will either win and convert them or else be converted themselves and grow comfortable with what is against God's Word and will. This turning away of the heart occurs gradually, and these people often argue that they are simply not trying to be judgmental of others.

Christ consciousness comes from the power of the Holy Spirit (Matthew 16:16–17), and it is the master key required to unlock God's Word and promises. Christ consciousness is the power to resist sin and follow after righteousness, no matter what Satan might try to lure you with. Satan can lure you with things that you take for granted such as making friends and associations. Christ consciousness is what will make you stand out in whatever you do and wherever you find yourself in this world.

As a good steward of God Most High, I strongly recommend putting the Lord into everything you are doing (Psalm 37:5; Proverbs 16:3). Putting your affairs into the hands of the Lord guarantees you success and divine favor. For God to fully bless, you are to submit totally in trust and obedience to his Word and instructions. This is what the Holy Spirit will teach you as you get closer and closer to knowing the Lord: to depend on his power. The quicker you learn that, the faster you will be promoted to the next level in the school of divine knowledge and understanding. Another point is that to retain the blessings that God has bestowed upon your life, your obedience to him must always be complete (2 Corinthians 2:9 & 10:6).

Satan (the devil) and the powers of darkness have blinded countless people in order that they should not believe or trust in God. In the last days people shall lose their love for the truth (Matthew 24:12) and will engage more in sin. In the last days a spiritual decrease in consciousness will abound as the love for holiness, righteousness, and purity declines. In the last days many people will go around preaching and teaching traditions and lies (Matthew 15:3–9). They will teach human tradition because it comes from and pleases the flesh (the natural man). They will teach lies because they are the seed of Satan to keep people from the truth and to confine them in darkness. The holy Bible states clearly that Satan's mission on earth is to kill, steal, and destroy, to divert men from obeying the Word of God, and to resist the Holy Spirit (the spirit of truth).

The Lord wants us as believers to rise above the power of tradition and customs, as they corrupt the truth. The power of tradition and customs hinders the power of the Holy Spirit. In such places where traditions and customs are made a big issue, the fire of prayer is not there. Whenever the power of God is not present, the power of darkness is able to work in that place. Wherever the power of God is not present, Satan will use people to resist the truth; and they will go against anyone who insists they do otherwise (**Matthew 24:9–10**).

Jeremiah 17:9 describes their "heart state" this way: "The heart is deceitful above all things, and desperately wicked: who can know it?" If the heart has been deceived, it becomes difficult to change that heart. In the medical-field, when the human heart has incurred some form of assault or damage, it can never be repaired. All that can be done is to maintain it until it is replaced by a whole new heart. In the spiritual, the transformation of transplanting a new heart can only be done by the spiritual Physician. Transplant and transforming can only take place when the spiritual heart is convicted through the power of the Holy Spirit.

Wickedness is one of the characteristics of Satan and the demonic powers. Wickedness abounds in the earth because of the falling away of many from the truth (tree of unrighteousness). As a result, the fruit they produce contains the seed(s) of Satan. The trees of unrighteousness harbor corruption, dissidence, and disobedience. Where there is no power of God in evidence, the people in that place perish. We as true believers in Jesus Christ are to pray for people who are walking in darkness. We are to pray that they may one day open their hearts and embrace the light. We are also to request through prayers for Jesus Christ to come into their life for transformation to take place. We as true believers are not to be self-centered, especially in the matter of prayer. Those who are selfish in their prayers must learn to be compassionate to those who have not received salvation. Jesus Christ said, "Those who are well do not need a physician" (see Matthew 9:12; Mark 2:17); therefore, healing is for those who are under satanic oppression.

With respect to those who don't believe in God and have continued in their wicked ways: "For he shall be like the heath in the desert and shall not see when good cometh; but shall inhabit the parched places in the wilderness, in a salt land and not inhabited" (Jeremiah 17:6). In that same chapter it is also written that "they shall not see good," because they are going against the will and word of God. Our God is holy and perfect; therefore, anything that goes contrary to God is unholy and imperfect.

In addition, going against the word of God, just as Satan did who was cast out of heaven, makes you an enemy of God. For these people God has prepared a place for his wrath to be unleashed. Many people are in the pathway of death, walking their way to destruction and completely oblivious. This is the deception of the heart, because Satan has blinded them so that they might not receive salvation and be delivered from the wrath of God to come. Satan and the power of darkness keeps these people in a lower state of spiritual consciousness. As stated earlier about the lower states of consciousness, some are born into it as infants and may never receive salvation. On the other hand, some people who were born into such a low state, after being saved, then make a conscious decision to return to that lower state. They choose spiritual sleep over spiritual wakefulness, as it looked pleasing and enticing. You must do everything to prevent yourself from going into such a lower state by being filled with the Holy Spirit. You have to be spiritually active to prevent spiritual sleep, through equipping yourself with the tools of the spirit (the armor of God).

One of the consequences of spiritual sleep or slumber is the inability to discern. When a believer loses connection with the power of God (the Holy Spirit), he or she begins to depend on human instincts as a guide for addressing daily running and activities. If you are a backslidden Christian, you are like a person walking in the light who suddenly finds himself in a dark room. In other words, a backslidden Christian is like a **person** walking with the light turned on over a dark path when suddenly the light goes out. Such is the description of a man going back and forth with sin and God. The Bible classifies such a person as lukewarm (Revelation 3:15–16). Such a person will never receive blessings from God and will never attain the full spiritual potential and heights that they should have attained just by trusting in the Lord. If you are such a person, I strongly encourage you today to make a conscious decision to wake up from that spiritual sleep and repent today. You are not playing a game of safety by going back and forth; rather, you are playing "the game of death" as spoken of by the Prophet Jeremiah (Jeremiah 17:6).

Another major problem with spiritual sleep or slumber is confusion in the last days. Confusion comes from not knowing who you are. Confusion arises in your life as a believer when the role you are to play in your walk with God, or your being in this world in general, remains a mystery. I have attended and taken part in many Christian crusades, and I have seen a great deal of street preaching and teaching. I daily thank God for giving me the opportunity to be a partaker of his promise and will.

The gospel is the intention of God, that Jesus Christ be preached all over the world. The intention of the gospel is also for accountability (**Matthew 24:14**). Accountability is the responsibility of all people as caretakers of the bodily vessels we possess. So we are held accountable for our actions and things we do with our bodies.

Your responsibility as a caretaker of God's vessel is to make sure that the body you possess may obtain salvation. Whether or not you are in some remote place, you will one day hear somebody speaking about Jesus Christ, God's promise, and the wrath to come. If you are reading this book and not yet saved, it behooves you to take out time and get saved.

Second, if you are not evangelizing, then you are not following Jesus Christ's last instructions to his disciples. A disciple is a steward who has been given a mandate to follow and do the will of his master. The will of God our maker is that we preach and share the good news. If salvation from God through Jesus Christ is based upon evangelism, you must never again say, "Let others do it." For this same reason Jesus Christ appeared to the Apostle Peter after his resurrection (John 21:15–17). Jesus asked Peter three times, "Simon, son of John, if you love me, feed my lambs … feed my sheep … If you love me, feed my sheep." I encourage you as a fellow steward and follower of Christ to take that bold step and speak about Jesus Christ to someone today. Do not think of what to say, as the Holy Spirit will fill your mouth with utterances to win that soul to Jesus Christ. He is the heart-surgeon to change that heart-of-stone to a heart-of-flesh

**(Ezekiel 11:19 & 36:26).** Don't struggle with him; let the Holy Spirit lead the way.

In the last days shall arise false prophets, teaching lies while using the Word of God to back up their agenda. The Bible states that by their fruit you shall know them. How can a true child of God resist and not be entangled with the spirits and powers of confusion of the last days? You must hold tight to the Word of God and instructions. The holy Bible says that matters (situations, scenarios, and conditions) should be considered, and the word of God should be your guide to addressing every doubt. Ephesians 4:14 states that we are to stand fast, and we are to be completely grounded (immersed) in our totality to the fullness of God's Word and power (Ephesians 6:11–13).

Simply put, God's intention for every true believer is that they should grow and attain spiritual maturity. Spiritual maturity means going into the higher stages of spiritual consciousness. Spiritual consciousness, in Christ Jesus, holds a power for sensitivity to life and security from anything that is contrary (confusion and chaos). I pray that you will continue to walk in that pathway of spiritual consciousness as it holds the promises of God in these last days.

> **Ye are all the children of light, and the children of the day: we are not of the night, nor of darkness. Therefore let us not sleep, as do others; but let us watch and be sober. For they that sleep sleep in the night; and they that be drunken are drunken in the night. But let us, who are of the day, be sober, putting on the breastplate of faith and love; and for an helmet, the hope of salvation. For**

**God hath not appointed us to wrath, but to obtain salvation by our Lord Jesus Christ, who died for us, that, whether we wake or sleep, we should live together with him. (1 Thessalonians 5:5–10)**

## $\mathcal{C}$orrupted Body Bring Forth Uncorruption

Jesus Christ is God in the flesh, and he came and dwelt among us, leaving all his power and glory behind, and came into this world in the similitude of a man. From what was written down by the apostles, who were with him during his ministry on Earth, they witnessed and testified that Jesus Christ was born in Judea; raised in Nazareth; crucified and buried in Jerusalem; and rose from the dead and ascended to heaven in the presence of his disciples and many others who witnessed it. From all this information recorded about him in the holy Bible, it can be concluded and affirmed that Jesus Christ, being born by a woman, was born into corruption, which is the body of human flesh. Everybody born into this world by a woman is born into the body of corruption. This follows from the fact that Adam and Eve in the Garden of Eden, although they were created by God uncorrupt, later became corrupt because of their disobedience and sin against God's rules, laws, and principles. God in his infinite wisdom did not want to destroy man as Satan (the serpent) intended; rather, he released a curse on man and the serpent (Satan).

God's intention for salvation to man is to bring out of the corrupted an uncorrupted body. This was strategically carried out, out of Satan's awareness. In addition, it was executed to defeat the power of death and for atonement for our sins, trespasses, and transgressions. Jesus Christ came into this world and did not yield his body to the power of spiritual corruption but kept himself pure and without sin. He did not sin against God because his divine assignment on Earth was to be sacrificed as the Lamb of God. As the sacrificial Lamb of God, he defeated the power of corruption that was brought upon man by sin and took all our curses upon himself. He not only took away all our curses but experienced God's wrath on the cross of Calvary. When he died, he took to the grave all our sin and left it there, buried forever, purging away all that was against us by his blood that was poured out.

Glory be to God in the highest! Jesus Christ rose from the grave on the third day and was transfigured from the corrupt to the uncorrupt. Because of his birth, crucifixion, death without sin, and resurrection, anybody who confesses their sin and accepts Jesus Christ as their Lord and Savior is saved (Romans 10:9). The benefit of salvation is that you are transformed by the power of God from the body of corruption to a body that is uncorrupted.

The power of transformation starts from within and works its way out. The inside-to-outside effect is that your soul and spiritual man will be empowered and revived to life. This is also meant to capture your conscience and help redirect your willpower, which is the power needed to make conscious decisions. As the power of God transforms you within, it cleanses your temple wherein lies the tower of spiritual control. The power of God cleans you from inside for the preparation and reception of the Holy Spirit. The power of God transforms you from the inside for your walk with God and for continuity of keeping your temple holy. God gave us his power and spirit, which is the Spirit of Truth and the light of God. The Spirit of

God can only dwell in a clean and holy temple. To retain the Holy Spirit, you must continue to exercise your spiritual gifts through praying and worshipping God.

Are you a believer and still working the acts of unrighteousness? Are you a believer who as a backslider thinks that God will never forgive you? Are you an unbeliever who has never accepted Jesus Christ into your life, or are you the one who prefers to remain on the fence of indecision? Are you a person who is living in fear? Are you a person who has taken an oath or done something else, and Satan is telling you that God will not forgive you? Are you a rapist, a murderer, a thief, a prostitute, a drug addict (or dealer), or involved in one or more habits that you think you can never stop? Are you feeling sad and lonely or contemplating suicide?

The Lord wants me to tell you that he loves you and to encourage you that you can change and be transformed from darkness (corruption) into a child of God (uncorrupted). All you need to do right now is to surrender your life to Jesus Christ. The decision to win starts from your heart. All you need to do is to allow Jesus Christ and the Holy Spirit into your heart and life today. God's promise to all of us is salvation and eternity in his kingdom. This is not a lie because everything about God's Word is confirmed by events you see around yourself and other people. You did not come into this world by mistake; everyone born on earth has a divine destiny and purpose. The only way to find your God-given purpose and ensure that your soul will be saved from the wrath of God to come, is to surrender your life to Jesus Christ today. If you want to give your life to Jesus Christ and be saved today; you must ask God for forgiveness for all your sins (confess all your sin).

**If you don't know how and what to pray, I advise you to pray this prayer with me today:**

> Father, in the name of Jesus Christ, I come into your presence with a humble heart and spirit, acknowledging and confessing all my sins, transgressions, trespasses, and iniquities. All these I put down and surrender to you, Lord Jesus. I believe that you will forgive me and not cast me away. I believe because your word in Roman 10:10 says, If I believe in my heart in you, I have been made righteous with God, and by confession with my mouth I am saved. I thank you, Lord Jesus, for the price you paid for me and affirm that you are my Lord and Savior. I thank you, Lord Jesus, for forgiving me and blotting out my curse and shame; and I ask that you write my name in the Book of Life. Thank you, Lord Jesus; thank you, Lord Jesus; thank you, Lord Jesus, Amen!

If you prayed that prayer, I encourage you to continue to walk with God and grow in the light of his power. First, I encourage you to get yourself a Bible, and start your reading from the book of the apostle John, and read straight through to Revelation. Second, I want you to join a true Bible-believing church and even become a worker in the house of God. Third, it's important for you to devote time daily to praying.

Last, and not least, ask your church leader about getting filled with the Holy Spirit. You need the impartation of the power of Holy Spirit to continue to grow and resist sin. You also need the power of the Holy Spirit to get a better understanding of the scriptures as you spend time reading them daily. I pray that the Lord keeps you from all troubles and that you may continue grow to know him. I pray that the Lord will lead you in the pathway of righteousness, so that at the end you are found worthy to enter his kingdom.

May the Lord our God bless you in Jesus Christ's name. Amen.

# 9

# *Facts about Spiritual Sleep in the Last Days*

### 1. The Wise and the Foolish Virgins (Matthew 25:1–13)

Jesus Christ used this parable to illustrate that those who are not prepared for his return will be like the foolish virgins. The only difference between the foolish and the wise virgins is their spiritual state of consciousness. The foolish virgins are believers who fall short in the matters of faith and trust.

The foolish virgins are asleep spiritually and have their consciousness impaired. The foolish virgins are the people who made a conscious decision to be asleep in the last days. They are believers who, while on Earth, pushed aside everything regarding their faith, belief, and spiritual life. Putting off the things of faith, they occupied themselves with the things that were unprofitable to their souls. This statement is confirmed because, upon the return of the Bridegroom (Jesus Christ), the foolish virgins will try to correct their shortcoming. They did not prepare themselves for the Last Days, which are going to be filled with darkness. When the darkness upon the earth is intensified in the pretribulation days, the Bridegroom will appear, and those virgins who are not prepared will be left behind.

Many people today are walking in the light of truth and have consciously made a right decision to keep their faith in Jesus Christ, no matter what the situation may be. This is a good example of the wise virgins. When the Bridegroom returns, the wise virgins are believers who have kept their anointing oil (the power of faith) bestowed upon them in their walk with God. The wise virgins are believers who keep their faith in Jesus Christ and do everything right to prevent themselves from being deceived.

## 2. The Book of Revelation and the Messages to the Seven Churches (Revelation 1–3)

The message to the seven churches was the vision from the Lord shown to the Apostle John. The churches are the body of Christ, and Jesus Christ is the head of the churches. Being a part of the body of Christ, we are expected to follow the spiritual rules, laws, and principles and the Word of God.

The Apostle Paul, in chapter two of the second epistle to Timothy, wrote: "The true soldier of Christ will not entangle himself with the affairs of this world" (paraphrasing verse 4). The message sent to the churches in the last days is to strengthen, warn, encourage, and edify the body of Christ. Jesus said his return will come like a thief in the night, and those who are asleep will not know when the return (rapture) is to take place.

The purpose of his return, as promised, is to take away those who have been faithful and kept themselves from corruption. Those who refused to follow the spiritual RLPs and the Word of God will be cast into the lake of fire for eternity. Those who wait on the Lord, as spoken by the prophet Isaiah, "shall mount up with wings as eagles; they shall run, and not be weary; they shall walk, and not faint" (Isaiah 40:31).

The promises of God are true because God is not a man that he should lie. He is a God of integrity and righteousness. Heaven and hell are for real, and they do exist. If they didn't exist, Jesus Christ wouldn't have made all those promises, even to return.

### 3. Hebrews 4:1–6, 9

> ¹*Therefore, since the promise of entering his rest still stands, let us be careful that none of you be found to have fallen short of it.* ²*For we also have had the good news proclaimed to us, just as they did; but the message they heard was of no value to them, because they did not share the faith of those who obeyed.* ³*Now we who have believed enter that rest, just as God has said, "So I declared on oath in my anger, 'They shall never enter my rest.'" And yet his works have been finished since the creation of the world.* ⁴*For somewhere he has spoken about the seventh day in these words: "On the seventh day God rested from all his works."* ⁵*And again in the passage above he says, "They shall never enter my rest."* ⁶*Therefore since it still remains for some to enter that rest, and since those who formerly had the good news proclaimed to them did not go in because of their disobedience, ... There remains, then, a Sabbath-rest for the people of God. (Hebrews 4:1–6, 9)*

The apostle Paul in the passage above is admonishing everybody who believes in Jesus Christ and is called to be a child of God to continue walking in the light of truth. Walking in the light of truth means becoming one with the light, which is becoming like Jesus Christ.

Walking in the light of Christ makes you into a tree of righteousness. When you are a tree of righteousness, you will only produce fruits that are good and not evil. This is true because everyone shall be held accountable on the ground of what they did on the earth. If you will be held accountable for everything you've done, whether good or bad, then it behooves you to do that which is acceptable to the Lord.

The children of darkness are not aware of this fact; even if they are, they continue in their wicked ways because they have been blinded from the truth. You, as a believer, one who is fully conscious about God and Jesus Christ, are expected to portray holiness in your behavior. When you fail to follow after Jesus Christ in this way, you automatically become an enemy of God. It is not worth it to do good in the beginning and turn bad at the end (see Ezekiel 18:1–32) and be excluded from the promises of God.

This is exactly what Apostle Paul was trying to say to you, to me, and to everybody walking in the light of truth. If you are in the light, there should be no darkness in you; neither should you bear fruits of unholiness in your substance.

The children of darkness go all out to fulfill whatever Satan requires of them. The majority of these people base their judgment, principles, and beliefs on natural human instincts rather than on Jesus Christ; and other on demonic influences. In other words, there are those who use supernatural powers to manipulate things in their favor or for the sake of destruction (being evil). Those who have sold their souls to Satan usually believe that they have nothing to lose. The truth is that they have something precious—their souls—which, according to the Word of God, will be cast into the lake of fire.

### 4. The Days of Great Tribulation (Matthew 24:29–31, 33)

In the days of great tribulation, according to Jesus Christ, many people shall fall from the pathway of truth. Many shall be lovers of themselves and will hate anything marked as holy. The days of the great tribulation are based on the return of Christ and the rapture. Hence, this time period is referred to as the post-rapture era.

The major event most notable to occur in that time is the leaving behind of those who are not found worthy to be raptured when Jesus Christ returns. Not to confuse the true facts about who will be raptured, some of those left behind will be Christians and born-again believers. Jesus warned that this time will be filled with events that have been prophesied and spoken of by the Prophets and by his Apostles. These facts are also highlighted in the book of Revelation, which was written by the Apostle John, and by the Prophet Isaiah (Isaiah 60).

This is not to fill you with apprehension but to create in you, as a true child of God, a holy fear. While natural fear will not lead you to fully yield yourself to the truth, holy fear brings forth righteousness. Belief and yielding are what spur you to love God with all your heart and make you seek after the truth. The truth sets you free and awakens you to the true nature and intention of God for your life and for every person in this world.

The intention of God is based on love; and this is why the Bible says that his banner over us is love (Song of Solomon 2:4). God has for us not just ordinary love but true love. For this reason, he sent his Son, Jesus Christ, to die for us to give us life and hope. The hope we have in God is in Jesus Christ. We hope for what is not seen now but for things to come. God has made provision for the things to come and will not disappoint.

He also sent his Son to forewarn us regarding the times that we find ourselves in today (pre-rapture) and the period of the great tribulation. The great tribulation will be observed by the believers and unbelievers who are spiritually asleep, including everybody who made a conscious decision to be asleep in the pre-rapture period. The period before and after the tribulation feature wars, pestilences, famine, and global hunger and hardship. Jesus Christ mentioned that at the time of the rapture, those who are left behind should flee to the mountains and hide; and those people left at home or in the farm should not return back inside the house to take items for their comfort but should flee away because they will be persecuted if they are Christians.

During the tribulation period God will pour out his wrath upon the earth, the heavenlies, and upon those who did not follow after the truth, righteousness, and holiness. On the other hand, those who are raptured with Jesus Christ will be with him in heaven and will behold the true nature of God. This is a beautiful sight not to miss, as we will also see the angels and all those we've read about in the Bible, as well as our loved ones who made it to heaven. We will all walk on the streets of gold and rest in our mansions as promised by Jesus Christ.

Jesus said (John 14:2–3): "in my father's house there are many mansions: if it were not so, I would have told you. I go to prepare a place for you. And if I go and prepare a place for you, I will come again, and receive you unto myself; that where I am, there ye may be also." In the next verse of that same chapter you will get a better understanding of the thought process and point of view of many believers and unbelievers. What these people are thinking about is something the devil is telling them, which is obviously intended to distort the truth. Satan is asking, "How can what has been written down in the Bible be real? And if it is real, will God fulfill this promise about heaven?" This clearly is the voice of Satan the deceiver.

Satan is the master of confusion. Even those who walked alongside Jesus Christ were still manipulated and deceived. In John 14:5, we read that the Apostle Thomas, one of Jesus's disciples, said to him: "Lord, we know not whither thou goest; and how can we know the way?" This shows that despite seeing the power of God being fulfilled as spoken and written by the prophets of old, Thomas portrayed doubt by questioning the credibility of Jesus Christ fulfilling God's Word.

In verse 8 of the same chapter, the Apostle Philip, another of Christ's disciples, demanded that Jesus Christ should "show [them] the Father, and it sufficeth us." Jesus Christ was disappointed and could not believe that after all the works and miracles that he had performed before them, they still did not believe, nor did they trust in his words.

## 5. The Last Days Will Be like the Days of Noah (Matthew 24:37–39)

Jesus Christ's return will be like the time of Noah in the Bible, because it shall come upon us unexpectedly. The question is why Jesus Christ decided to use the days of Noah as an example. God told Noah that he would destroy the earth and said he should go out to the people to tell them about God's intention. The people laughed and thought it impossible for God to destroy every breathing thing upon the earth. As we analyze and compare the time of Noah to what is going on around us now, we see that the inhabitants of the earth at that time were corrupted and disobedient. In addition, there was increased shedding of innocent blood and cries of bloodshed going up to heaven. In addition, they did not believe in Noah for their souls to be saved because Satan had blinded them from awakening to the truth.

Similarly, in the time of the prophet Jeremiah, God sent him to the people of Judah and the king, urging them to repent because of their sins and disobedience. The people of Judah had turned their back on God and sought help from other gods by making for themselves idols. They also worshipped strange gods of the people of Canaan, who were destroyed by God. God sent many prophets, pastors, and messengers, but they did not listen to them.

Similarly, in this present period, God has sent many messengers and has given us signs for the pre-rapture, and pretribulation era. The difference between this era and Noah's time is that God's intention now is to destroy the earth and the heaven and to bring a new heaven and earth. God's intention is to return everything back to its original design and order in which everything was created. Second, God's intention is to bring an end to Satan and the powers of darkness, which is peace forevermore. "Glory to God in the highest, and on earth peace, good will toward men" (Luke 2:14).

## *6. Revelation 21:7–8*

> He that overcometh shall inherit all things; and I will be his God, and he shall be my son. But the fearful, and unbelieving, and the abominable, and murderers, and whoremongers, and sorcerers, and idolaters, and all liars, shall have

their part in the lake which burneth with fire and
brimstone: which is the second death.

Here are two of the perennial questions on these subjects:
"When will all these things written in the scripture take place?"
and "Who will experience the wrath of God?" Revelation 21:7–8
contains a list of people who will be cast into the lake which
burns with fire and brimstone. As stated earlier, this is not meant
to terrorize but to create in your heart a holy fear. Holy fear
produces in a believer the power to retain and to demonstrate
holiness and righteousness (and abstain from the opposite).
Holiness is key because our God is a holy God; and those who
worship shall worship him in spirit and in truth (holiness).
Second, our God is a righteous God, and we are his children, so
we ought to be like our Father. We are expected to operate at the
level of righteousness.

As proven by scientific research, the genes of the father are
passed to his child and expressed through several processes to
create that child. The genetic makeup of a child dictates the
child's phenotypical (physiological) makeup. If we are the
children of God, then we are to act like him. Jesus Christ said,
"What I see my Father do, that I do also" (see John 5:19), and
stated in John 14:11, "Believe me that I am in the Father, and the
Father in me: or else believe me for the very works' sake."

The fear of God is the beginning of wisdom, and those who
obey his word have understanding (see Psalm 111:10). I would
like you to look at two words here: *wisdom* and *understanding*.
This clearly is telling you that if you fear God, you have wisdom;
and if you obey God's Word, you have understanding. The power
for wisdom and understanding comes from God. The power for
expressing spiritual understanding and wisdom, as they are both

qualities of the Spirit of God, comes from the Holy Spirit. Hence, in Proverbs 7, King Solomon speaks about having the Holy Spirit, and the need to incorporate (engage) him into everything we do as the children of God. Wisdom and understanding teach us to love God and trust him and his Son (Jesus Christ).

Wisdom and understanding teach you to desire God's power, which can be found only when you receive the Holy Spirit. The Holy Spirit helps you so that you know your God and walk in the light of his power, which is Jesus Christ. Jesus said, "I am the way, the truth, and the life" (John 14:6), and Proverbs says, "Whoever finds [wisdom] finds life" (8:35 NKJV).

The Holy Spirit guides you and helps you stay in the pathway to eternal life and salvation. To remain in the pathway of life, you must yield yourself to the Holy Spirit and not sin. Those who remain in the pathway of righteousness shall have eternal life and shall be saved from the second death.

Another important thing to bear in mind is that Jesus Christ did set a standard on who will be saved from the wrath of God to come. For you to enter the kingdom of God, your righteousness must exceed that of the Pharisees (see Matthew 5:20).

### 7. Matthew 24:44–51

> Therefore be ye also ready: for in such an hour as ye think not the Son of man cometh.
>
> Who then is a faithful and wise servant, whom his lord hath made ruler over his household, to give them meat in due season? Blessed is that servant, whom his lord when he cometh shall find so doing. Verily I say unto you, That he shall make him ruler over all his goods. But and if that evil servant shall say in his heart, My lord

delayeth his coming; and shall begin to smite his fellowservants, and to eat and drink with the drunken; the lord of that servant shall come in a day when he looketh not for him, and in an hour that he is not aware of, and shall cut him asunder, and appoint him his portion with the hypocrites: there shall be weeping and gnashing of teeth.

The steward that the Lord shall meet doing the works of righteousness shall be rewarded. Those who have kept their bodies from sin, transgression, and unholiness shall be blessed. These are the people marked to meet the criteria for being raptured according to the Bible. God's intention is to put an end to evil and to restore all things to the state in which they were first created. Satan did bring corruption, and according to the Holy Scriptures, his ending shall be reckoned with the ending of sin and disobedience. Those who followed him will all be cast into the lake of fire.

## 8. The Day of Separation of the Sheep from the Goats (Matthew 25:31–46)

When the Son of man shall come in his glory, and all the holy angels with him, then shall he sit upon the throne of his glory: and before him shall be gathered all nations: and he shall separate them one from another, as a shepherd divideth his sheep from the goats: and he shall set the sheep on his right hand, but the goats on the left.

Then shall the King say unto them on his right hand, Come, ye blessed of my Father, inherit the kingdom prepared for you from the foundation of the world: for I was an hungred, and ye gave me meat: I was thirsty, and ye gave me drink: I was a stranger, and ye took me in: naked, and ye clothed me: I was sick, and ye visited me: I was in prison, and ye came unto me.

Then shall the righteous answer him, saying, Lord, when saw we thee an hungred, and fed thee? or thirsty, and gave thee drink? When saw we thee a stranger, and took thee in? or naked, and clothed thee? Or when saw we thee sick, or in prison, and came unto thee?

And the King shall answer and say unto them, Verily I say unto you, Inasmuch as ye have done it unto one of the least of these my brethren, ye have done it unto me.

Then shall he say also unto them on the left hand, Depart from me, ye cursed, into everlasting fire, prepared for the devil and his angels: For I was an hungred, and ye gave me no meat: I was thirsty, and ye gave me no drink: I was a stranger, and ye took me not in: naked, and ye clothed me not: sick, and in prison, and ye visited me not.

Then shall they also answer him, saying, Lord, when saw we thee an hungred, or athirst, or a stranger, or naked, or sick, or in prison, and did not minister unto thee?

Then shall he answer them, saying, Verily I say unto you, Inasmuch as ye did it not to one of the least of these, ye did it not to me.

And these shall go away into everlasting punishment: but the righteous into life eternal.

God is in the business of promoting and establishing his children for outstanding greatness. Greatness and honor come from the Lord. In regard to greatness and honor, I don't mean earthly achievements or accomplishments. I want you to know that God also blesses with earthly riches and wealth; let nobody tell you differently. Our God is the king and owner of the universe, including the hidden treasures; all of these belong to him. This is the reason why the Bible calls those who put their trust in earthly riches, but not in the Lord, as lost and set for destruction.

God's desire is that all souls may be saved and not destroyed. Sadly, sins and disobedience make it hard to seek after righteousness and truth. Many cannot find their way to the truth because the truth demands holiness and righteousness. Many people don't want anything to do with what will reveal their true nature to them. They are afraid of seeing themselves for who they really are in nature. Many people are afraid to face their weakness and fears and would rather give in to sin than overwhelm themselves with their true nature.

The power of disobedience works in every one of us to a certain degree; however, there are people who have taken time out to put the power (human nature) under the control of the power of God. That power of God now working in their lives sank roots into their hearts when they opened them up and embraced the truth. That truth is the light of God's power (Jesus Christ). The light of God's power has illuminated and enlightened their life; beneficently, they are transformed through that light into children of the light.

The process described here is spiritual regeneration. Praise be to God because through the light coming into believers' lives, all their true nature and all the old things are brought to the point of acknowledgment. Acknowledgment is key to the period of spiritual awakening. Remember that spiritual awakening is taking place because of the light of Christ working within you. In addition, the acknowledging period being empowered by the power of Christ, your regenerated heart allows you to see things for yourself, because the light of God's power has awakened your senses from spiritual sleep.

Awakening and seeing the truth is the beginning of salvation because it pushes you into thorough repentance from your old ways. Repentance is the process of separating and turning away from sin. The process that leads from acknowledgment to repentance described here is called the transformation from a goat into a sheep.

When I was a young boy, we used to have almost seventy goats. I did spend a lot of time observing, feeding, and cleaning up after them. Goats are some of the smartest and stubbornest animals you will ever come across. Just like people, each and every one has a distinct character. Goats are just as intelligent as dogs. They can do specific tricks, surprisingly without being trained. Another thing about goats is that they are noisy and sometimes greedy. A well-known fact about goats is that they eat anything, except their raw meat, and themselves.

Taking a looking at the physical nature of goats and sheep, they almost look alike, except for the color and texture of their coats. Goats tend to be more aggressive and uncooperative. You can walk sheep but not goats, as they will not follow you. Goats cannot be taken for a long-distance unleashed, because they will go their own way, and the goatherd will lose more than two-thirds of those he went out with.

Sheep can stay together without fighting each other, but goats will always fight each other for food, even amid abundance. In abundance they will quickly eat what is given to them and pounce on the weak ones to eat their food. Goats will fight each other for the most comfortable space in the field, even though there is plenty of space.

Moving from the description of natural goats and sheep to the spiritual goat and sheep, we must ask, what is the moral behind Jesus Christ's parable? Jesus used sheep and goats to illustrate how the children of God will be separated from those who did not believe in God's Son, Jesus Christ.

Spiritual goats, just like natural goats, fear nothing and have no fear of God in their heart. The spiritual goats are greedy, lustful, selfish, disobedient, murderers, fornicators, adulterers, homosexuals, thieves, gossips, liars, haters, racists, unholy, despisers of truth and righteousness, and lovers of bribes. The goats are so many in our world today because of increased disobedience.

Goats are easily distractible and quick to forget. Spiritual goats will not follow the goatherd and easily get lost. When goats are lost, they quickly forget where they were coming from and will soon lose their love for the truth. Just as natural goats will never listen to or follow the goatherd, so also spiritual goats will not follow after Jesus Christ (the true shepherd). Some goats may follow at a certain distance but will soon get bored; in addition, some will also be distracted by something along the way and eventually take their own path.

Spiritual goats are unruly and will never follow after God. As a result of their actions they will be punished for their straying away. Spiritual goats will be punished for yielding to lies and seductions. This is the reason why as a believer, being counted as a sheep, in your actions you must endeavor to maintain your spiritual sanity and purity. You must keep yourself under the shadow of the Shepherd, following after righteousness.

Jesus Christ said: "I am the true good shepherd" (see John 10:11–16). Only the shepherd knows the way back home and will defend his sheep from wild beasts. The sheep follows after its master because there is something bonding them. That bonding between the sheep and the shepherd is grounded in love and trust.

Jesus Christ said, "I lay down my life for my sheep. I give away my life for my sheep because I love my sheep" (amplifying John 10:15). This is true because Jesus Christ was crucified upon the cross of Calvary for everybody, and he rose again and ascended into heaven. Upon ascending to heaven, he did not abandon us in this world but sent to us a guide, a teacher, and a comforter.

When he shall return to judge the world, we will all stand before him to give account of what we did on earth. According to the vision of John in the book of Revelation, two books will be opened before the Lord. Those whose names are not written in these books according to our Lord are the spiritual goats. The consequence of those who name is not written is eternal condemnation in the wrath of God.

Those whose names are written in the books are the spiritual sheep and will enter into eternal rest and peace in heaven. This should be everybody's dream who walks on the face of the earth. We are to fear the Lord and not do anything to sell ourselves cheaply because of sin or lust. I encourage you today to walk in the light and likeness of the Shepherd, and you will never be ashamed at the end. God bless you now and forever … *Amen.*

**Elohim Our God Ministries.**
**Pastor A. I. Uzebu**

# About the Author

A. I. Uzebu is the founder of Elohim Our God Ministries in Chicago. He was called by God to fulfill some specific assignment for the body of Christ in the last days. An aspiring physician, he wants to inspire those in the light to keep it on and those in darkness to come to the light **to depopulate the kingdom of darkness while following God's word wholeheartedly.**

Printed in the United States
By Bookmasters